To Andrey and Dean.
with love.

Dennis and Ros.

A
Suffolk
Christmas

To John Burke,
who has left Suffolk,
and to
Louis Hipperson,
who has returned

A
Suffolk
Christmas

Compiled by Humphrey Phelps

ALAN SUTTON PUBLISHING LIMITED

First published in the United Kingdom in 1991
Alan Sutton Publishing Limited · Phoenix Mill · Far Thrupp
Stroud · Gloucestershire

Reprinted 1995

British Library Cataloguing in Publication Data

Phelps, Humphrey
A Suffolk Christmas.
I. Title
820.8033

ISBN 0-86299-979-0

Cover illustration: Christmas Eve delivering presents, *by
William Erasmus Jones (courtesy of N.R. Omell Gallery;
photograph: Fine Art Photographic Library Limited)*

Typeset in Garamond 12/13.
Typesetting and origination by
Alan Sutton Publishing Limited.
Printed in Great Britain by
WBC Ltd, Bridgend.

Contents

v

· *A Suffolk Christmas* ·

· A Suffolk Christmas ·

· A Suffolk Christmas ·

· A Suffolk Christmas ·

Friston mill

Christmas 1863

CLIFFORD MORSLEY

*Born at Chelmsford in 1920, Clifford Morsley spent most
of his boyhood in the Leiston district where his family had
been living since 1723. In 1940 he enlisted in the Suffolk
Regiment. He now lives at Reydon.*

How was Christmas celebrated in the 'good old days' and,
particularly, how was it enjoyed in the good old county of
Suffolk? Some of the answers to these questions are to be found
in musty, yellowing records of 1863, which tell of festivities
in Suffolk towns and some of the larger villages exactly a
century ago.

The weather was not of the traditional variety. In fact, on
the great day itself, at North Cover, near Beccles, strawberries
were in blossom and in one garden they were almost ready for
picking. But a few days later there was a sharp frost and the
Waveney at Beccles was crowded with skaters. There were
many skaters, too, on the fishpond at Abbots Hall, Stowmarket. Here they enjoyed themselves until long after dark, in
the light of many torches. These ringed the pond at the
expense of Mr William Prentice, who owned Abbots Hall.

In the 1860s Stowmarket was famous for its annual
'Provision Show' arranged by the butchers of the town. In
1863 it was held just a couple of weeks before Christmas Day
and said to be the best ever. Mr Meadows in his shop in the
Market Place, exhibited the largest bullock killed in the town

that year, a beast of 100 stones which had been bred by Mr King of Desnich Hall, Newmarket – 'and the quality of the meat and smallness of the bone was remarkable'. It was flanked by two more of its kind which came from the farm of Mr Stearn of Stowupland. Grouped around them were 'ten wonderfully fine quality half bred sheep'. All were displayed in a forest of evergreens and right in the centre, above Mr King's prize bullock, was a picture of the beast in life, with a crown over its head.

Mr Cuthbert of Bury Street had two monster sheep in the centre of his window, each weighing about 300 lbs. His prize exhibits in beef were three 'home-breds' grazed by the Revd W.H. Crawford of Haughley. The shop was illuminated by gas-jets and through their help fire belched through the nostrils of the principal ox. Two other butchers, Mr Fairweather and Mrs Rush, made their appeal to folk who liked a piece of pork for the Christmas spread and showed massive joints which were surrounded by garlands of mistletoe. Mr Colson had a large show of poultry, including 200 turkeys, many geese, 400 pheasants, patridges and hares. He also introduced grouse to the Stowmarket Christmas show for the first time.

A week after the show, the Stowmarket people enjoyed another of their annual Christmas events. This was the distribution of coats and gowns for the elderly poor. As for many years past and for years to come, these were given away by the fiefs of the Stowmarket charities and the Churchwardens.

In Ipswich on Christmas Eve the shops and streets were crowded and business was brisk until a very late hour. A brass band played in the open air until midnight and there were many parties of carollers and 'waits'. Mr C.J. Meadows, furnisher and general ironmonger of Tavern Street, gave his staff a supper and convivial evening. Appropriately it was held at the Great White Horse, so well remembered by that very great lover of Christmas festivities, Mr Charles Dickens, whose *Christmas Carol* had appeared only twenty years previously. A few days later, Messrs Harris and Gislingham, upholsterers, gave a supper to their workpeople; this was held in their own premises in Museum Street.

One of the people who attended the Stowmarket provision show pointed out that the goods on display were for those with long purses and hoped that the poor would not be forgotten. His hopes were realized in most of the villages through gifts by the squire, the parson and the farmers. At Earsham Hall lived Capt. Meade who was 'ever ready to remember the indigent and to sustain the character of a fine Old English Gentleman'. In the week before Christmas he saw that every cottager in his district had a good fire for he gave away 15 tons of coal. Mrs Meade bought 75 blankets for distribution in the village.

At Tendring the Revd Mr Chapman and some of his more wealthy parishioners saw that 25 tons of coal were supplied to homes where money was scarce. Squire Long of Hurts Hall,

Saxmundham, slaughtered two bullocks to provide Christmas dinners for old people. And neither were the inmates of the workhouse forgotten. On Christmas Day – a Friday that year – the Guardians of Blything Union provided 'a bountiful repast consisting of good old English cheer'. The chaplain, genial Parson Noott, and a Mr Burleigh presented each man with a pint of 'genuine Stout', Mr W.H. Aldred saw that the men also had a gift of tobacco, and snuff, tea and oranges were passed around generally.

In Stowmarket – surely no town had more of the Christmas spirit that year – there was a tea for all men and women who were over 55 years of age and connected with the parish church. The County Court was given over to the feast and carefully disguised in an abundance of holly and fir. On the walls were very large banners with inscriptions, one reminding the subscribers that 'He who gives to the Poor, lendest to the Lord'.

On Christmas morning most folk went to church. Scole church had been well-known for its seasonable decorations for several years and evidently maintained its reputation in 1863. Sentences of scripture were formed with green leaves against a background of scarlet cloth – and there were wreaths of holly and 'mottoes and other devices'. Much praise for their excellence was given to a young lady – Miss Wimberley. At Woodbridge this style of decoration was sufficiently new to recall painful memories of times when great bushes were stuck along the tops of pews. These had resulted in scratched faces and torn dresses and had almost shut out any view of the parson as he preached the Christmas sermon.

On an evening shortly after Christmas, on 29 December, some of the Hadleigh people and others in the surrounding villages were brought to their doors by the noise of drums and bugles. As many of the marchers were carrying flaming torches, some of the oldest inhabitants might well have

thought that Napoleon had landed after all, in the way he promised in the days when they were young. The commotion was actually caused by the Volunteers, 11th Suffolk Rifles, on the march from Hadleigh to Monks Eleigh to have supper with Mr Robert Hawkins.

They needed the torches because the night was very dark — and it was very wet as well. After their six mile walk in bad weather they had excellent appetites for their very good meal. Afterwards they toasted their host and his wife, their Commanding Officer, Lieut. Robinson, and many other people beside. They finished the evening by singing 'God save the Queen' and 'then returned to their respective homes'. Understandably, perhaps, there is no mention of a march back to Hadleigh.

The poor in some parishes received annual gifts on New Year's Day, under ancient bequests. One such village was Great Ashfield where the widows each received a quarter-pound of tea, a pound of sugar, a slice of plum cake and a glass of gin. For the widowers there were a couple of sovereigns from Mr Chapman of Ashfield Hall. On New Year's Day at Ipswich, the churchwardens of St Mary Key distributed about '100 stones' of bread and £4 in cash among the aged poor. At Helmingham the Sunday School children of the parish church attended morning service and then went along to the rectory. Each youngster received 'a good large bun' for refreshment and some clothing for the cold months ahead. Some of the boys had new shirts and jackets as gifts and others were given a pair of 'trowsers'.

At another village nearby, the Revd C.J. Cornish entertained some of the old people at the parsonage. Those who were too old to attend had 'a good substantial dinner' sent to them in their own homes. The Tendring parson gave his widows and widowers a New Year's Dinner and a tea. Those who lived any distance from the rectory were taken to the feasting in the rector's carriage and they had a ride home as well.

Christmas Market

ADRIAN BELL

*Adrian Bell went as a pupil to a west Suffolk farm in
1920. It was still a time of high farming in Suffolk, and
Christmas fatstock sales were a great occasion in the
farming year. In this piece, taken from* Corduroy, *Bell's
first book, he gives his impressions of the 1920 Christmas
sale at Bury St Edmunds which he called Stambury. Mr
Colville, his mentor, expresses the traditional large
farmer's dislike of poultry.*

The next Wednesday was Christmas sale day at Stambury, and
Mr Colville took me with him to see it. The town was full of
cars and farmers. Inn yards were crowded with gigs. The
market-place was at one end of the town, a vast space divided
up into pens and selling-rings under cover.

Dealers hailed Mr Colville near the entrance with, 'I've got a
pretty bunch of heifers this morning that would just suit you,
sir,' and 'Do you want to see some real fine beasts, now?'

'They're Irishmen,' he said. 'They bring Irish cattle over,
and rough ones too, sometimes. The trouble is, the Irish won't
pay enough attention to quality – they use any old bull. But
the cattle are hardy. There was an old chap who used to farm in
a big way near here; as mean as could be, he was. He'd buy
fifty Irish cattle, and all he'd give them to eat through the
winter was barley straw. They used to come out of the yards in
the spring looking like scarecrows. He was the luckiest old

Fat Red Poll bullocks, native cattle of Suffolk

man on God's earth – if they'd belonged to anyone else half of them would have died. It was wonderful how they pulled together, though, on the grass when they were turned out.'

There was a great bustle of unloading, penning, and marking the creatures. A variety of gross persons with sticks were driving cattle about the alleyways between the pens shouting, 'Mind your back – hup-ho! hup-ho!' Whichever way I turned I seemed to find a herd of bullocks charging down upon me.

The pens near the rings contained the fat beasts, and were garnished with holly and laurel. A piece of mistletoe (some-body's joke) dangled over the auctioneer's head. The prize cattle wore rosettes, and cards were tied to their pens with 'First Prize', 'Second Prize', 'Highly Commended' printed on them. The first prizewinner, a red Shorthorn steer, was a breath-bating spectacle as he strode round the ring, supreme in width and depth. He was like a creature of legend sublimated in the telling.

So was the second, snow-white and classical – Europa's own. A man with gold rings in his ears having a woman of lascivious curves tattooed upon his arm urged him round.

'There,' said Mr Colville, 'How would you like a joint off him for your Christmas dinner?'

The auctioneer, searching the throng with keen eyes, enumerated the bids. Old men fingered their beards, pronouncing judgement on this year's quality. The bidders, simulating unconcern, nodding imperceptibly, shot occasional quick glances to spot their rivals. It was a battle royal of butchers for the prestige of having a carcase with a red rosette hanging in their shops, a carcase split, showing inner qualities of meat and fat corresponding to those outward proportions for which he had been famous. Butchers who cater for farmers have a clientele of connoisseurs, and at Christmas time something extra special is expected.

'Turkeys be damned,' said Mr Colville before this brave show of creatures, 'give me beef and plum pudding'.

What, indeed, was turkey to him, who had pheasants or partridge for the aiming of his gun? Not cooked in 'camera' in an oven either, but turning upon a spit close above brilliant wood embers on the old hearth in the scullery, well basted, hissing and browning, their flavours sealed within them. His wife kept turkeys for the Christmas trade; all day at Farley Hall their melancholy calling filled the air.

'Their row gets on my nerves,' said Mr Colville more than once. 'Thank God when they're sold and gone. I don't want to see one again for a long while, least of all on Christmas Day.'

The first prize steer made £85, the second £80. 'A tidy price, but they won't forget to charge us when we want a joint,' said Mr Colville.

Seasonal Fare and Handbells

GEORGE EWART EVANS

George Ewart Evans was a pioneer of oral history and wrote an impressive number of books on Suffolk. Here, in his last book, Spoken History, published shortly before his death, two men reminisce about Christmas past. The first, George Messenger, worked at Snape Maltings, the second, Robert Sherwood, was a farmer at Blaxhall.

George Messenger:
A man named Lord Renlesham fatted a bullock every year. There was a pound for father and a pound for mother and half a pound for each of us children: we were seven. He gave us a pound of sugar and a pound of plums [raisins] and half a pound of beef suet, so we could have a pudding. We would have got no Christmas dinner but for that, unless we'd got a rabbit or two. That was at Christmas time: the other part of the time the poor old lady sometimes she ain't got much for us to eat. She'd get some bread and she'd go to the fire and she'd get hold of the kittle, and cut the bread up and had some salt and pepper and she'd pour hot water on it. There you go! Kittle-broth. Sometimes we'd go to the shop for tea. Three pence an ounce it was then. We used to have an ounce of green tea and an ounce of black tea. Mix them together. That would last a week. If you

A Suffolk bull

fell short at the end of the week, you'd get some bread, put it before the fire and make it black, and put it in a big mug, pour hot water on it; and call it coffee. That's how we used to go on.

Robert Sherwood:
They [the handbell-ringers] used to visit all the farmhouses and places in Blaxhall, and I remember when they came up to mine at Lime Tree Farm. First of all they'd ring outside in the porch one or two times; and then my wife and I used to ask them in. And they used to come into the dining-room and, I remember, we always had to put a very thick cloth on the table. They used to stand round the dining-room table and ring the hand-bells and occasionally they put them down on the cloth, and it used to change them in some way. The object was that the cloth was put there so the bells wouldn't vibrate. As soon as they put a bell down it was dead. Of course, we knew them all personally and when they finished they had

mugs of beer. And of course we always gave them something in the way of moneykind. And it was a most enjoyable evening and an occasion that was looked forward to. Absolutely! We always expected them.

Christmas Husbandrie Fare

THOMAS TUSSER

Thomas Tusser (c.1524–80) farmed for a time at Cattiwade in the Stour Valley. While farming there he wrote the first version of his Points of Good Husbandry. *Though unsuccessful as a farmer, his book in doggerel verse contains much sound advice and many of his lines are now regarded as proverbs. His original* A Hundred Points *was later expanded to* Five Hundred Points *together with the* Points of Housewiferie.

Good husband and huswife now cheefly be glad,
　　things handsom to have, as they ought to be had;
They both doo provide against Christmas doo come,
　　to welcome good neighbour, good cheere to have some.

Goode bread and good drinke, a good fier in the hall,
　　brawne, pudding and souse, and good mustard withall.

Donkeys at Summerhill, Leiston

Beefe, mutton, and porke, shred pieces of the best,
  pig, veale, goose and capon, and turkey well drest;
Cheese, apples and nuts, joly Carols to heare,
  as then in the countrie is counted good cheare.

What cost to good husband is any of this?
  good household provision onely it is.
Of other the like, I doo leave out a menie,
  that costeth the husbandman never a penie.

Ploughing

B.A. STEWARD

B.A. Steward had a small farm in Suffolk and was also the Daily Herald's *agricultural correspondent. In this extract from* Farm down the Lane, *it is wartime, Christmas is approaching, and the ploughing must be completed.*

Behind the two-furrow plough the earth turns over in heavy smooth square slabs, like liver, chocolate brown. They gleam in the pale winter's sunlight as if there were a vein of silver in the clay.

And Jim on the tractor leans back in his seat and presses the lever that lifts out the plough-breasts as he sweeps round once again on the headlands of Little Smithies, the five acre field that borders one boundary of the farm.

He is alone, except for the company of pee-wits and gulls, and a wagtail that has followed him up and down the furrows. For Sam is several fields away, with his horses Captain and Honey, drawing out the first furrows in a field on the other slope of the hill.

They both have an urgent task.

For Christmas is coming. Jim is reminded of it by the old holly tree, with its clusters of red berries, that now beckons him like a beacon from the hedge, where it has shone like a kindly light for so many ploughmen, now forgotten, in dark and wintry days gone by.

The tree is gnarled and deformed, but the berries never fail.

· A Suffolk Christmas ·

Ploughing by the ruin of All Saints, Dunwich

They say that Old Johnny, who farmed this land so many years ago, walked down here every Christmas Eve and took branches from the tree to an all-night celebration with a friend who farmed the neighbouring farm.

They celebrated not only 'peace on earth', but also the fact that both of them had finished all their ploughing by Christmas Day.

Part of Johnny's celebrations – so the story goes – was to polish the breast of his plough and put it under his bed on Christmas Eve. At least, that was what every good farmer on heavy land was supposed to do.

And that, or something like it, is what Sam and Jim are trying to do now.

They know, just as well as Old Johnny, the difference that it will make to the spring sowings and to next year's harvest. For winter's frosts and thaws will temper these furrows and break down this stubborn clay and, when spring comes, the teeth of the cromes will tear and rake the earth unto what is called a tilth, a mellow tilth, for the barley seeding.

14

Over the valley, on other farms, men and horses are ploughing, and the tractors roar. They are at war against their ancient enemy, Time, and his ally, the Weather.

So far, this year, it has been touch and go. On many wet undrained fields the work is held up. On many farms the heaps of sugar-beet lie out uncarted in the puddled fields. Thousands of acres of winter wheat are still unsown.

But Jim now moves out of the gateway and the five acres of Little Smithies lie stretched out in the glory of their fresh shimmering dark brown furrows.

Another field ploughed. And behind him the old holly tree gleams red in the sunset, a promise of peace on earth again and that all this work on the farms will in due time be done.

from

Pickwick Papers

CHARLES DICKENS

'And numerous indeed are the hearts to which Christmas brings a brief season of happiness and enjoyment,' wrote Charles Dickens in Pickwick Papers. And numerous too are the hearts to which Pickwick Papers has brought enjoyment. Sufficient excuse, if excuse be needed, to include some brief extracts from the accounts of Mr Pickwick's visits to Sudbury, Bury St Edmunds, and Ipswich.

As a young reporter on the Morning Chronicle,

The annual Boxing Day hunt meet at Angel Hill, Bury St Edmunds in 1990 (*East Anglian Daily Times*)

Charles Dickens often visited Suffolk to report on elections. He stayed at the Great White Horse Hotel, Ipswich, which he described in Pickwick Papers, *causing the landlord to threaten him with libel action. It was also at Ipswich on 31 December 1861 that Dickens gave the last of his famous readings.*

Dickens was coy about the location and identity of the place called Eatanswill, saying he had been unable to find it on any county map. But he knew that the real name of Eatanswill was the town of Sudbury, with an election in progress.

Bribing and nobbling opponents were some of the methods used in elections. Electioneers 'persuaded' voters to support their candidates and Sudbury in particular had a notorious reputation for corruption and violence. Pick-wick Papers *was initially published in monthly parts between April 1836 and November 1837 before the state*

· A Suffolk Christmas ·

of affairs at Sudbury came to a head. In 1841, the two elected candidates were unseated and proceedings were started for the disenfranchisement of the borough because of the corrupt practices during the general election.

It was late in the evening when Mr Pickwick and his companions, assisted by Sam, dismounted from the roof of the Eatanswill coach. Large blue silk flags were flying from the windows of the Town Arms Inn, and bills were posted in every sash, intimating in gigantic letters, that the honourable Samuel Slumkey's Committee sat there daily. A crowd of idlers were assembled in the road, looking at a hoarse man in the balcony, who was apparently talking himself very red in the face on Mr Slumkey's behalf; but the force and point of whose arguments were somewhat impaired by the perpetual beating of four large drums which Mr Fitzkin's committee had stationed at the street corner . . .

. . . The Pickwickians had no sooner dismounted, than they were surrounded by a branch mob of the honest and independent, who forthwith set up three deafening cheers, which being responded to by the main body (for it's not at all necessary for a crowd to know what they are cheering about) swelled into a tremendous roar of triumph, which stopped even the red-faced man in the balcony.

'Hurrah!' shouted the mob in conclusion.

'One cheer more,' screamed the little fugle man in the balcony, and out shouted the mob again, as if lungs were cast iron with steel works.

'Slumkey for ever,' yelled the honest and independent.

'Slumkey for ever!' echoed Mr Pickwick, taking off his hat.

'No, Fitzkin!' roared the crowd.

'Certainly not!' shouted Mr Pickwick.

'Hurrah!' And then there was another roaring like that of a whole menagerie when the elephant has rung the bell for the cold meat.

'Who is Slumkey?' whispered Mr Tupman.

'I don't know,' replied Mr Pickwick in the same tone. 'Hush. Don't ask any questions. It's always best on these occasions to do what the mob do.'

'But suppose there are two mobs,' suggested Mr Snodgrass.

'Shout with the largest,' replied Mr Pickwick. . . .

Leaving Sudbury, Mr Pickwick then went to the place that William Cobbett called, 'The nicest town in the world.'. . .

'Beg your pardon, Sir,' said Sam, suddenly breaking off in his loquacious discourse. 'Is this Bury St Edmunds?'

'It is,' replied Mr Pickwick.

The coach rattled through the well-paved streets of a handsome little town, of thriving and cleanly appearance, and stopped before a large inn situated in a wide open street, nearly facing the old abbey.

'And this,' said Mr Pickwick looking up, 'is the Angel! We alight here, Sam. But some caution is necessary. Order a private room, and do not mention my name. You understand.' . . .

'Now, Sam,' said Mr Pickwick, 'the first thing to be done is to —'

'Order dinner, Sir,' interposed Mr Weller. 'It's very late, sir.'

'Ah, so it is,' said Mr Pickwick, looking at his watch. 'You are right, Sam.'. . .

'Leave that to me, sir,' said Sam. 'Let me order you a snug little dinner, and make any inquiries below while it's a getting ready; I could worm ev'ry secret out o' the boots' heart, in five minutes, sir.'

'Do so,' said Mr Pickwick: and Mr Weller at once retired.

In half an hour, Mr Pickwick was seated at a very satisfactory dinner . . .

In the main street of Ipswich, on the left-hand side of the way, a short distance after you have passed through the open space fronting the Town Hall, stands an inn known far and wide by the appellation of the Great White Horse, rendered the more

conspicuous by a stone statue of some rapacious animal with flowing mane and tail, distantly resembling an insane cart-horse, which is elevated above the principal door. The Great White Horse is famous in the neighbourhood, in the same degree as a prize ox, or county paper-chronicled turnip, or unwieldy pig – for its enormous size. Never were such labyrinths of uncarpeted passages, such clusters of mouldy, ill-lighted rooms, such huge numbers of small dens for eating or sleeping in, beneath any one roof, as are collected together between the four walls of the Great White Horse at Ipswich.

It was at the door of this overgrown tavern that the London coach stopped, at the same hour every evening; and it was from the same London coach, that Mr Pickwick, Sam Weller and Mr Peter Magnus dismounted, on the particular evening to which this chapter of our history bears reference . . .

Much later Mr Pickwick lost his way in the hotel. Leaving his bedroom he went downstairs and the more stairs he went down, the more stairs there seemed to be to descend, and again and again. Not surprisingly, on his return he was unable to find his bedroom. Eventually he found what he thought was his room, undressed and got into bed.

Mr Pickwick almost fainted with horror and dismay. Standing before the dressing-glass was a middle-aged lady, in yellow curl-papers, busily engaged in brushing what ladies call their 'back-hair'. However the unconscious middle-aged lady came into that room, it was quite clear that she contemplated remaining there for the night; for she had brought a rush light and shade with her, which, with praiseworthy precautions against fire, she had stationed in a basin on the floor, where it was glimmering away, like a gigantic lighthouse in a particularly small piece of water.

'Bless my soul,' thought Mr Pickwick, 'what a dreadful thing!'

'Hem!' said the lady and in went Mr Pickwick's head with automaton-like rapidity.

'I never met with anything so awful as this,' thought poor Mr Pickwick, the cold perspiration starting in drops upon his night-cap. 'Never. This is fearful.'

It was quite impossible to resist the urgent desire to see what was going forward. So out went Mr Pickwick's head again. The prospect was worse than before. The middle-aged lady had finished arranging her hair; had carefully enveloped it in a muslin night-cap with a small plaited border; and was gazing pensively on the fire.

'This matter is growing alarming,' reasoned Mr Pickwick with himself. 'I can't allow things to go on in this way. By the self-possession of that lady, it is clear to me that I must have come into the wrong room. If I call out she'll alarm the house; but if I remain here the consequences will be still more frightful.'

Trouble at Bulcamp

ALAN IVIMEY

The nineteenth century was a particularly hard time for the rural poor. By the 1834 Poor Law Amendment Act, outdoor relief was practically abolished and those unfortunates unable to support themselves were accepted into

workhouses after subjection to the 'workhouse test'. Condi-
tions in workhouses were deliberately made unpleasant in
order to encourage inmates to go out and find work.

The Blything Workhouse at Bulcamp catered for
several parishes and its site is now occupied by the
Blythburgh and District Hospital.

There were cases at Bulcamp of couples marrying and going
straight to the Workhouse to live, their children in due course
living as young paupers. These would be apprenticed or 'put
out to service' and then return to the Workhouse, marry and
have pauper children. At one time there were three generations
of such paupers at Bulcamp. The Directors' answer to this was
to try and separate men and women, husbands and wives in
different parts of the building. And then the trouble started.

In December 1835 the Guardians heard that a mob armed
with picks, crowbars and other useful implements were
advancing upon Bulcamp from several directions. Urgent
messages for help were sent out. Southwold refused to have

Bulcamp workhouse, 1880s

anything to do with the affair but a van arrived from Wangford 'filled with persons willing to be sworn in as Special Constables' while others arrived from Halesworth.

Then the mob, which seems to have taken its time, though about two hundred strong, appeared advancing along the Halesworth road. The valiant guardians, with three local magistrates, took their stand at the gate and read the Riot Act to the rioters who then moved off, making threatening noises and promising to return with a larger force. This they never did, probably because they heard that the military had been sent for from Ipswich. But some of the inmates had become excited and one particularly formidable wife from Westleton (we only know that her Christian name was Rachel and that her husband's name was Joseph) had broken down part of the workhouse walls with a poker. She was to be taken before the Earl of Stradbroke and dealt with 'according to law'.

Christmas is Seldom White

EAST ANGLIAN DAILY TIMES

A white Christmas, so much talked about, is a rarity in East Anglia where since 1788 only ten really snowy Christmases have occurred, with only three of these in the present century.

The first white Christmas of the century was in 1906, when

snow began falling late on 25 December. It continued all night and by noon on Boxing Day depths of about twelve inches were reported on level ground with drifts of up to six feet in exposed rural districts.

The next white Christmas of the century was during the memorable blizzard of 25–6 December 1927, which ranked as one of the worst on record. Soon after 6 p.m. on Christmas Day, continuous rain over Suffolk and Essex turned to snow.

This became so heavy over the country that by midnight hundreds of main roads were blocked and in the Salisbury Plain area some drifts were more than 15 feet deep. . . .

The last snow on Christmas Day occurred in 1938. Most of Suffolk and Essex was snow covered on Christmas Eve, and in the ensuing 24 hours north-easterly gales brought further snow inland from the North Sea. Floating ice was observed in the River Stour.

Between 1780 and 1880 white Christmases were comparatively frequent in East Anglia. There was deep snow and severe frost on Christmas Day 1796, and in Ipswich a Doctor

Aldeburgh Moot Hall

23

Hamilton recorded a temperature of two degrees Fahrenheit (30 degrees of frost) in his garden on Christmas morning. White Christmases occurred in East Anglia in 1788, 1798, 1830, 1836, 1840, 1870 and 1874.

Despite tradition and the unrelenting efforts of Christmas card designers, widespread snow and severe frost are rarely experienced during the last week of December. This is due to the marked tendency for mild, stormy weather from the Atlantic to occur at or about this time. . . .

Climatological statistics reveal that during the last 50 years, unsettled weather with a predominance of strong winds and rain has occurred on 44 occasions. The Scandinavian and Russian anti-cyclones, which usually bring East Anglia its coldest weather, normally begin their westward movement after Christmas.

The severest month for several centuries was January 1814, when the last 'frost fair' took place on the icebound River Thames.

Tragedy at Sea

DOROTHY THOMPSON

Dorothy Thompson was the daughter of the Reverend Henry Thompson who became the vicar of Aldeburgh in 1874. This story illustrates the dangers which face the fishermen and lifeboat crews of the Suffolk coast and is in sharp contrast to the usual scenes associated with Christmas.

24

Packing herrings, Lowestoft, *c.* 1910

On 7 December 1899, the sprat boats which had taken the early morning tide had realized a gale was brewing, and beached at a village further north. When the storm broke, a gale raged from the east dead on shore. About 11 a.m. minute guns were heard firing out at sea and the lifeboat, *The Aldeburgh*, was called out to a vessel in distress off the Sunk light. The regular lifeboat coxswain, James Cable, had been ill, and was only up for the first time, but meant to occupy his usual place in the boat. However, the doctor knew his man, and he arrived at his house in time to prevent him leaving it. While he was arguing the case, the boat was launched; the second coxswain was also ill, but an experienced seaman who had been coxswain of a previous lifeboat took command. The usual competition for belts had taken place, eighteen men had donned them, and the crew were in their places. The boat was warped off in the usual way; it was a rough day, but not by any means one of the worst storms or heaviest seas the boat had encountered. There had been a little delay over deciding if the boat was to go, and when it was launched the tide was three parts flood, which was bad for getting her away. The sails were set, and the wind was strong, and when she was on the inner shoal for the final dash through the waves breaking on it, a mighty sea struck her on her broadside, and before the helm could recover she was over, in sight of the watchers on the shore. A great cry of horror rose from the crowded beach. The boat did not sink, but was driven, keel uppermost, towards the shore. The men were good swimmers, but the waves rolled them and battered them, and when pulled on shore by rescuers on the beach, in some cases artificial respiration had to be given, and in one case, though the doctor worked for an hour, it was useless. There was roll-call, and five men were missing, and it was realized that they were under the boat. Up to their necks in icy waters in the breakers the rescuers worked, being directed by the regular coxswain, who now refused to be held back by sickness but stood in the water working as hard as anyone. They could not raise the boat; they tried hacking a hole in her, it was hard work, she was so well built, and when they had done it they still could not get to the imprisoned men. It was not until the tide went down, and the boat was raised with levers and screwjacks, and the shingle dug out on one side, that one of the bodies was recovered. The women had gone back to their cottages, and Henry went to each one, and found them waiting for husbands' and sons' last homecoming.

The vicar was presiding at a school managers' meeting in his study, when the door was burst open by his youngest daughter to tell them of the awful tragedy she had witnessed. The managers went at once to the beach to help, while Henry went to minister to the sorrowing. Some of them were young wives with babies, whose brave husbands were in full strength of their fine manhood. They risked their lives in the work of rescue, knowing full well that some day the supreme sacrifice might be accepted from them, but the town was stunned by the blow when it came. That evening the little street was deserted, the inhabitants sat behind closed doors, mourning.

All through the night before the funeral the snow fell softly, and the churchyard was covered with a pure-white glistening carpet; paths had to be swept and sanded, but all around lay the white pall. Business was suspended, shops shut, flags flown at half-mast. One by one, the six coffins, covered with Union Jacks, were borne on hand biers from their cottage homes into the main street. The lifeboat crew in life belts and scarlet caps were ready to receive them and act as pall bearers. Coastguards and volunteers formed up, and the local band, playing the Dead March, lead the procession. At the bottom of the Church hill there was a brief halt to allow the Major and Corporation to take their places in the procession. Up the hill to the old flint church at the top it wended its way, the Union

A lifeboat being launched from Aldeburgh

Jacks, scarlet caps and Mayor's robe, making bright patches of colour in the snow-clad world. Arrived at the church door, the procession opened out, and Henry's clear voice could be heard in the still air, reciting the opening sentences. Slowly the six coffins were carried into Church by the mates of the men who had come for the last time to the Church where they had been baptized, had worshipped, and all but one, been married.

The graves were dug in the sailors' corner of the burial ground, and after the singing of the hymn 'Jesu, Lover of my Soul' the men were carried to their last resting-place in sound of the sea, and with a view of waves breaking on a distant point.

Ipswich Drinking Song

ANON

Bryng us in no browne bred, fore that is made of brane,
Not bryng us in no whyt bred, for therein is no game;
But bryng us in good ale.

Bryng us in no befe, for ther is many bonys [bones],
But bryng us in good ale, for that goth downe at onys
[once],
And bryng us in good ale.

· A Suffolk Christmas ·

Bryng us in no bacon, for that is passing fate,
But bryng us in good ale, and gyfe is i-nough of that;
And bryng us in good ale.

Bryng us in no mutton, for that is often lene,
Nor bring us in no trypes, for thei be syldom clene;
But bryng us in good ale.

Bryng us in no eggs, for ther ar many schelles,
But bryng us in good ale, and gyfe us no[th]yng ellys;
And bryng us in good ale.

Bryng us in no butter, for therin ar many herys [hairs],
Nor bryng us in no pygges flesch, for that wyl mak us
    borys;
But bryng us in good ale.

29

Bryng us in no podynges, for therein is al Godes good,
Nor bryng us in no venesen, for that is not for owr blod;
But bryng us in good ale.

Bryng us in no capons flesch, for that is oft der,
Nor bryng us in no dokes [duck's] flesch, for thei slober in
the mer [mire];
But bryng us in good ale.

A Southwold Christmas

LYN KNIGHTS

Lyn Knights now runs the old established and respected outfitters Denny & Son in the Market Place at Southwold. A ghost is reputed to haunt the premises. On several occasions footsteps have been heard in an upstairs room which, on investigation, has always proved to be unoccupied. But this ghost has never been heard at Christmas time; although on Christmas Day when the shop is closed, it may be dancing a Christmas jig.

Christmas is magic, it was especially so when I was a small child, as my father John W. Denny was a leading light in preparing the Christmas decorations.

· *A Suffolk Christmas* ·

Decorations in the Market Place, Southwold

In 1953 the chalet was made, complete with Father Christmas, reindeer and sleigh. Every night, visiting choirs and schools sang carols, and bands played. About four years later the castle was built. This was an amazing feat and took up most of the Market Place. Nightly the town was packed, as bands played and various schools and choirs sang well known carols, often accompanied by the crowds.

Today the tradition still continues, not on quite such a grand scale, but still the atmosphere is electric.

Father Christmas and his fairy appear as it gets dark. First we hear the band, then Father Christmas arrives – this year (1990) on top of an open bus. Sweets are thrown and balloons released as he climbs the stairs of the Town Hall. Once on the balcony all the lights are turned on, making Southwold a riot of colour. The band strikes up and carols are played and sung. Christmas has arrived. Soon it is time for Santa to visit his grotto and the children rush forward to join the queue.

My small son was heard to say to Father Christmas, 'Hello Joe,' only to be told to 'hurry along, son'. He was later heard to complain, 'And he didn't even ask me what I wanted for Christmas.'

Each year Father Christmas arrives in some different form of transport – a beautiful stage coach and four, an open vintage Bentley, and he has even been pulled along on a cart by the entire Rugby team.

The switching on of the Christmas lights is sometimes accompanied by late-night shopping – another 'not to be missed' occasion, even in Southwold. The hospitality is generous with all the shops, banks and hotels supplying endless wine and hot mince pies, the staff dressed in some amazing creations. There is a prize for the best dressed windows and the most original clothes.

Letter from Boulge

EDWARD FITZGERALD

Edward Fitzgerald was born at Bredfield in 1809 and is best known for his translation into English verse of The Rubáiyát of *Omar Khayyám. At various times he lived at Boulge, Faringay Hall, and, after the break-up of his marriage, Woodbridge.*

Among his literary friends with whom he corresponded were Thomas Carlyle, W.M. Thackeray, Alfred, Lord Tennyson, and his elder brother Frederic, who was also a poet. Here is part of a long letter written on 8 December 1844 at Boulge and addressed to Frederic Tennyson.

· *A Suffolk Christmas* ·

My Dear Frederic,

What is a poor devil to do? You tell me quite truly that my letters have not two ideas in them, and yet you tell me to write my two ideas as soon as I can. So indeed it is so far easy to write down one's two ideas, if they are not very abstruse ones; but then what the devil encouragement is it to a poor fellow to expose his nakedness so? All I can say is, to say again that if you lived in this place, you would not write so long a letter as you have done, full of capital description and all good things; though without any compliment I am not sure you would write better than I shall. But you see the original fault in me is that I choose to be in such a place as this at all; that argues certainly a talent for dullness which no situation, nor intercourse of men could much improve. It is true; I really do like to sit in this doleful place with a good fire, a cat and dog on the rug, and an old woman in the kitchen. This is all my live stock. The house is yet damp as last year; and the great event of this winter is my putting up a trough round the eaves to carry off the wet. There was discussion whether the trough should be of iron or of zinc: iron dear and lasting and zinc the reverse. It was decided for iron, and accordingly iron is put up . . .'

PS Next morning. Snow over the ground. We have our wonders of inundation in Suffolk also, I can tell you. For three weeks ago such floods came, that an old woman was carried off as she was retiring from a beer house about 9 p.m., and drowned. She was probably half seas over before she left the beer house.

And three nights ago I looked out at about ten o'clock at night, before going to bed. It seemed perfectly still; frosty, and the stars shining bright. I heard a continuous moaning sound, which I knew to be, not that of an infant exposed, or female ravished, but of the sea, more than ten miles off! What little wind there was carried to us the murmurs of the waves

circulating round these coasts so far over a flat country. But people here think that this sound so heard is not from the waves that break, but a kind of prophetic voice from the body of the sea itself announcing great gales. Sure enough we have got them, however heralded. Now I say that all this shows that we in Suffolk are not so completely given over to prose and turnips as some would have us. I always said that being near the sea, and being able to catch a glimpse of it from the tops of hills, and of houses, redeemed Suffolk from dullness; and at all events that our turnip fields, dull in themselves; were at least set all around with an undeniably poetic element.

from

'The Farmer's Boy'

ROBERT BLOOMFIELD

Robert Bloomfield, the pastoral poet, was born at Honington on 3 December 1766 and when a boy worked on a farm at Sapiston. 'The Farmer's Boy', his best known poem, was published in 1800 and twenty-six thousand copies were sold in the succeeding three years. He died, however, in poverty in 1823.

Him, though the cold may pierce, and storms molest,
Succeeding hours shall cheer with warmth and rest;
Gladness to spread, and raise the grateful smile,

· A Suffolk Christmas ·

He hurls the faggot bursting from the pile,
And many a log and rifted trunk conveys,
To heap the fire, and wide extend the blaze,
That quivering strong through every opening flies,
Whilst smoky columns unobstructed rise.
For the rude architect, unknown to fame,
(Nor symmetry nor elegance his aim)
Who spreads his floors of solid oak on high,
On beams rough-hewn, from age to age that lie,
Bade his wide fabric unimpair'd sustain
Pomona's store, and cheese, and golden grain;
Bade, from its central base, capacious laid,
The well-wrought chimney rear its lofty head;
Where since hath many a savoury ham been stor'd,
And tempests howl'd, and Christmas gambols roar'd.

Flat on the hearth the glowing embers lie,
And flames reflected dance in every eye:
There the long billet forced at last to bend,

While gushing sap froths out at either end,
Throws round its welcome heat:– the ploughman smiles,
And oft the joke runs hard on sheepish Giles,
Who sits joint tenant of the corner-stool,
The converse sharing, through in duty's school;
For now attentively 'tis his to hear
Interrogations from the Master's chair.

Ghost in the Garden

H. MILLS WEST

*Suffolk has an abundance of ghosts but very few of them seem
to be active at Christmas, or if they are their activities have
not been recorded. Fortunately, Mr West has provided us
with one which did manifest at Christmas.*

*H. Mills West left school at fourteen and went to work on
the land. Seven years later he was offered a place at a small
college for agricultural workers. Many years later, after
another period working on the land, he again went to college
and he taught in country schools for twenty-five years.*

I forget what it was that took me to see old Ben Collis on that
wild night just before last Christmas. Perhaps it was only
because, being fellow villagers for over a generation, we

Lavenham, one of the weaving towns of Suffolk

sometimes shared a bottle towards the end of the year and swapped anecdotes of years gone by. But I think now that it was something more positive than chance that took me there on that particular night.

What I remember, only too clearly, is that there was someone coming from Ben's house when I arrived. Not that I took much notice at the time – it was dark and cold and there was a vicious sleet in the air that kept peoples' heads down and their eyes on the ground. Nevertheless, when I opened the garden gate to go in, a figure was standing there as reasonably clearly as one would expect in that weather. In fact, he stood aside for a moment – a man, certainly – and I thanked him for his courtesy and went up to the house. I had the impression that he stood there for a few seconds in the darkness, then the gate slammed and he was gone.

It was a minute or two before there was any answer to my

knocking. The unlit house and the encounter with the figure
at the gate gave me a chilling feeling that all was not right.
Then, just as I was about to leave, a light came on, and then
another – the whole house came to life again – and old Ben was
standing in the doorway as hearty and welcoming as ever.

'You've had a visitor already,' I remarked, following him to
a seat in front of a roaring fire. Old Ben sat down and poked at
the logs till the sparks flew, absorbed in the pleasure of
warmth and company, and I could not be sure that he had
heard. At his age he could not be expected to hear and respond
to every chance remark. Anyway, it was none of my business
and I forgot the matter. We had a game of draughts as was our
custom but the game was so drawn out, what with drinking
and telling tales, that we often forgot who had moved last.
Then the game was over or abandoned and Ben was searching
through a box of old photographs.

I could not help noticing, as he brought a handful of
pictures towards the firelight, that he had changed a good deal
since I had seen him a year before, a change not only in
appearance but in his behaviour. Perhaps, I thought, it was
simply the mark of old age, certainly he seemed more
forgetful, so distant sometimes that he had to rouse himself to
come back to the present.

'Tha's some-whoile, I can tell ye, since I had a look at these
owd things,' he was saying. 'I allust reckon tha's like raisin'
owd ghosts when yew go lookin' up peoples' likenesses o' long
ago. But there's someone here I want yew to hev a look at.'

He began to shuffle through the photographs then seemed
to remember a phrase he had just used. 'Do yew believe in
ghosts?' he asked suddenly. I would have laughed but for his
serious tone and the memory of the sinister-looking figure at
the gate. 'Produce one and I'll believe in it,' I promised him.

'Well, 'haps I will. Now do yew look at this hare picture.
Whew dew that remind yew of?' It was of a wedding couple. It

took me a minute or two to recognize that the handsome young bridegroom was Ben himself as a young man.

'Well, I never knew –' I began to utter surprise. Ben was saying in a voice distant with thoughts of the past, 'jest look at her face. Ain't she a proper good-lookin' gal?'

'Never knew you were ever married,' I finished, staring at the picture.

'Am married,' he corrected me. 'Poor Bess – she's still alive in one of them mental hospitals. She 'on't come out no more. She don't even remember me. She know me jest as someone who go an' visit her sometimes an' take little presents. She look forward to them visits – arter all, tha's the only thing she can look forward tew.'

Up to now old Ben seemed to have been fighting against tiredness but now a sudden note of urgency made his voice strong and insistent as he pleaded:

'Anything happen ter me – will yew go an' see what yew can dew for the poor owd gal? Jest go an' say hullo, take a bunch o' flowers, anything. Jest so she got somebody – so she don't fare left out.' He handed me a scribbled address. 'I reckon yew'd dew that for me – ef that so happened that way.' His voice was so earnest I promised solemnly that I would go regularly to see his wife should his own visits be brought to an end. He seemed immediately to be pacified and his head began to nod again before the warm fire.

But at the back of my mind I was still bothered, not by his request which I was quite happy to agree to but at my own memory of that dark, ominous figure outside and at his earlier pointed question: 'Do you believe in ghosts?'

'What was the name of your visitor?' I asked him, but there was no answer. I thought I must have tired the old man out. Very quietly I collected my hat and coat and was starting towards the door when he roused himself and muttered as if in a sleep – 'Don't yew forget what yew promised.'

'I won't,' I said, and left him sitting there in the familiar posture with the firelight throwing shadows across his face. I came out of the door into the cold, blustery wind that brought the chimes of midnight in jagged snatches to my ears.

Halfway down the garden path I came to a sudden startled halt. At the gate was the same dark figure that I had seen before. To what ghostly vigil was this apparition committed? But it was moving now and coming towards me, seemingly immensely tall and powerful — this time it was I who stood rooted to the spot. The figure came nearer, and put itself close in front of me, and spoke:

'What are you doing here?' it asked, in a brisk but everyday sort of voice reminiscent of the local constable. 'Perhaps you'd like to tell me how it is you're just coming away from that house?'

It took me all of a minute to take in the questions, to come back to the world of ordinary mortals and to realize that in fact this really was the village constable. I could not help noticing that he was almost as startled as I was.

'Phew,' I breathed in relief. 'Thank heaven you're real. It's all right about my being here — I've been to see old Ben. You know, when I saw you at the gate for the second time I thought I was seeing a ghost.'

'I think you were,' the constable answered, coming closer to stare into my face, 'if you spent the evening in that house.'

'I don't understand,' I said. 'Why were you watching the cottage? Is Ben Collis in any kind of trouble?'

'You could say so,' the policeman answered shortly. 'Come and have a look.'

With an uneasy feeling in the pit of my stomach, I followed him back to the door I had just left. The cottage looked dark and silent and unwelcoming. 'Gone to bed,' I surmised, shivering, 'and I don't think we should wake him without good reason. Do you mind telling me what you are doing here?'

'Certainly, I will,' the policeman answered in a low tone.

'There's no mystery about why I'm here. I'm keeping an eye on an empty house.'

I stared. 'But I played draughts with Ben – we had a drink, talked. In fact he made a particular request that I should visit his wife if he should die.'

'There's a lot of questions here that I can't answer,' the law admitted soberly. 'Perhaps they're the sort that don't have an answer, not a rational one. There may be something in the idea that the spirit is sometimes strong enough to do miracles. I reckon he hung on somehow so he could give you that message to look after his wife. Let's look inside.'

It was not the cold that made me shiver as I went into the cottage again. It needed but a glance to see that the room where we had sat was empty, the fire long ago cold – a room where no one lived.

'The old man was killed in a road accident earlier today,' the constable said.

Fog by the Shore

GEORGE CRABBE

George Crabbe was born at Aldeburgh on Christmas Eve, 1754, the son of a salt tax collector. His birthplace has since been washed away by the sea. He was educated at Bungay and Stowmarket, apprenticed to an apothecary at Aldeburgh and later practised as a doctor to a garrison of soldiers in the town. Later he was ordained at Norwich and in 1781 returned to Aldeburgh as curate at the parish church.

· A Suffolk Christmas ·

A catch of herrings, Lowestoft

The ocean too has winter views serene,
When all you see through densest fog is seen;
When you can hear the fishers near at hand
Distinctly speak, you see not where they stand;
Or sometimes them and not their boats discern,
Or half-conceal'd some figure at the stern;
The view's all bounded, and from side to side
Your utmost prospect but a few ells wide . . .
'Tis pleasant then to view the nets float past,
Net after net till you have seen the last;
And as you wait till all beyond you slip,
A boat comes sliding from an anchor'd ship,
Breaking the silence with the dipping oar,
And their own tones, as labouring for the shore,
Those measured tones which with the scene agree,
And give a sadness to serenity.

Seasonal Customs

CLIFFORD MORSLEY

For very many years the Christmas dinner was immediately followed by the ceremony of the Wassail Bowl. In some parts of the country the bowl contained highly-spiced wines with apples afloat on the surface, but in the homes of the farmers it more generally brimmed with ale, to which they added sugar and nutmeg, ginger and toast. Whatever the concoction, the ceremony followed traditional lines, the host wishing 'Merry Christmas' to all his guests and then stirring the beverage before taking first pull. The bowl was then sent round the board, and served as a signal for the singing of Yuletide songs.

Good cheer did not, of course, begin and end on Christmas Day. Not the least of the festivities were the markets and fairs, where folk gathered to sell their cattle and poultry, and, in the evenings, to enjoy themselves. One Suffolk hamlet, Coldfair Green, near Leiston, actually got its name from the annual fair, which took place there on a stretch of grassland, on the 11th and 12th days of cold December. The fair was held annually for hundreds of years, and continued up to comparatively recent times. In later years there were boxing booths, roundabouts, a small circus and the like. Fortune-tellers came from a tribe of gypsies who had winter encampment in Knodishall, about a quarter of a mile from the fairground. In the district one may still hear the adage: 'A light cold fair and a dark Christmas'.

In some parts of the country one of the first rites for

Christmas Day involved the boiling of the Hackin or great sausage, which was served with strong beer and cheese. If the sausage had not been boiled by daybreak, two young men were sent to seize the cook and run her round the market-place, as penance for her idleness. Later in the day, as a prelude to their dinner, the village youngsters took off their coats, tied their shirtsleeves with ribbons, and decorated their hats with Christmas foliage. They then performed country dances while another boy, with a fox skin pulled over his head, capered and jumped along the onlookers, offering a collecting-box.

Another custom sent the Suffolk boys in search of owls and squirrels on Christmas Day, in accordance with observances which were still being observed in Bury St Edmund's 150 years ago. One writer tells of similar hunts in Ireland, where wrens were killed and fastened to broomsticks festooned in holly and ivy. In the evening the lads, carrying the broomsticks, went in procession around the farms to obtain rewards in money and nuts.

In the days of the watchman, Christmas greetings and jingles were delivered as a 'follow-up' to such familiar cries as 'three of the clock and a fine night'. In the morning the watchman called round again, rang their bells and asked for a gift.

Coaching Days

LEONARD P. THOMPSON

Leonard Philip Thompson (1907–87) was born in Ipswich, educated locally, and trained as a reporter with the Woodbridge Reporter, *eventually becoming managing director of the family building firm. He wrote many articles for local publications, and several books which included:* Tales of Old Ipswich, Smugglers of the Suffolk Coast, *and* Inns of the Suffolk Coast. *This piece is from* Suffolk Coaching Days.

During the week before Christmas, 1836, the weather was exceptionally mild. In some Ipswich gardens, crocuses and snowdrops were making an unusually early appearance. At Nacton, someone picked violets. The sun shone as people went about the cheerful business of preparing for a Christmastide which promised to be more spring-like than wintry.

But England was about to be gripped by the most severe weather it had known since 1799. During Thursday 22 December, the weather became cooler. The wind veered from south to east-north-east. The next day was very cold, and during the evening there was a light fall of snow, followed by a sharp frost. People who were going to travel some distance to spend Christmas with families and friends, and had taken the precaution of booking their seats well in advance of the busiest coaching period of the year began to contemplate their journeys with mixed feelings. Many of them remembered the

· A Suffolk Christmas ·

The mail coach

severe frost which had made coach travel so hazardous on Christmas Eve, 1830.

By the early hours of the morning of 24 December, Ipswich was blanketed in snow. Coach passengers, who had slept at the Great White Horse overnight to be ready for the early departure, stamped their feet and swung their arms as ostlers brought horses down Northgate Street from the inn's great range of stables which covered the site now occupied by Neale Street.

It was a brave Christmas-card scene which Tavern Street presented early on that morning of Christmas Eve, 1836. Ostlers lanterns, coach lamps, and lights from the Great White Horse windows were reflected on the snow in faintly glowing patches of amber streaked with pale rose. The horses, rosetted, their collars and heads sprigged with holly, subjected patiently to the operation of being harnessed. Mistletoe hung from the red-painted sides of the coach; geese and turkeys festooned from every possible point, and the roof was piled with hampers; more hampers were suspended beneath the coach, between the axle-trees. When all was ready the coachman sporting a bunch of 'Christmas' in the button-hole of his many caped coat, came out of the inn, cheerful, confident, warmed no doubt by hot brandy-and-water.

The snow fell more heavily, and those who climbed aboard the coach began to have misgivings as to whether they would in fact spend Christmas among their families; their fears as events were to show, were only too well founded.

On Christmas Day, blizzards piled the snow into drifts of frightening magnitude. Great, blue-white ridges, 80 feet in breadth and from 10 to 14 feet high, were reported on the outskirts of Ipswich. All roads leading from the town were impassable. At many points of the important Norwich, Bury and Yarmouth turn-pikes, snow lay higher than the roofs of the stranded coaches. As the snow-muffled bells called the people of Ipswich to the Christmas service, several of the families who ventured through the deeply-covered streets to church were incomplete. Somewhere, far beyond the town, among the great white wastes that now stretched over the whole of the country, were loved ones who would not be home for Christmas.

Some of the travellers did not fare too badly. Those fortunate enough to have a journey interrupted near an inn, found shelter, warmth and sustenance. Some even found a measure of entertainment. Certainly the passengers of several coaches that were held up at Dunchurch, on the Holyhead road, made the best of their plight. Between them, they filled the Dun Cow and the Green Man. The first morning, someone organized a shoot – two guns among sixteen sportsmen. Jack Goodwin, guard of the Manchester coach 'Bee-Hive' secured the only bag – a hare. That evening the landlord of the Dun Cow organized a dancing party. Next morning, the irrepressible Goodwin formed a choir, which visited such nearby farmhouses as could be reached, where the carollers were entertained with elderberry wine and pork pies.

On Christmas night, the Norwich mail set out from the Royal Hotel in a brave attempt to make the long journey to London via Ipswich; it sank into a ridge of snow near the city and could not be extricated. But it was an inflexible rule, as well as a proud tradition, that His Majesty's mails must get through, and the Christmas mail eventually was brought into Ipswich by a post-chaise and four horses on the evening of Wednesday 28 December.

Watts, guard of the Yarmouth mail, arrived in Ipswich on the Tuesday evening in a vehicle drawn by two horses in tandem. He had been nearly lost in the snow near Corton [near Lowestoft], but had been rescued by three men. Wet through, tired almost to the point of dropping, and without a change of clothing, he left Ipswich with the mail bags for London the same evening.

The Ipswich mail coach, which should have reached Norwich on Christmas Day, did not pull in until 11 o'clock on Wednesday night. It had managed to get as far as Thwaite Buck's Head [near Eye] whence the letter bags had been dispatched in the charge of mounted messengers. One of the passengers, Capt. Petre, undertook to walk to Norwich, a distance of 28 miles; he arrived in the city on the 28th, and thence proceeded on his journey to Westwick House.

On Monday morning another mail coach attempted the journey from Ipswich to Norwich, but its progress became completely blocked at Barham [near Ipswich], and the horses broke their traces. The guard, with considerable difficulty, reached Thwaite, but there he found it impossible to proceed any further. Like so many travellers before and since, he was grateful for the hospitality of the Buck's Head. The Bury coach also left Ipswich on the Monday morning but had to stop at

Claydon [near Ipswich]; the passengers made their way back to Ipswich as best they could. The same day the 'Phenomena' down coach from London to Norwich had to abandon its journey at Sudbury.

It was not until New Year's Eve, when snow still lay two feet deep in the streets of Ipswich, that the coaches were able to get to Norwich; a hastily recruited army of 400 men had cut a passage for them through the drifts.

Green Lane Farm in the 1940s

B.A. STEWARD

I have always liked a goose for Christmas, but in future I shall settle for a nice piece of pork, thank you. Not that I don't still prefer goose. I like the look of them as fluffy yellow goslings. I admire them when I see them doing the goose step over the green. The one that I select looks even better when it comes steaming out of the oven.

But this year some subversive influence seems to have come over everybody in the village. There are still a few who will pluck turkeys, but nobody who will pluck a goose.

What Old Nart refers to admiringly as the 'real old women' no longer want the job of sitting with a bath in front of them, in a room where you can see nothing but feathers. The young ones say that it makes such a mess in the house.

· A Suffolk Christmas ·

After I had made such an unavailing tour of Lesser Snoring with bottles of beer and other gifts as bribes I was forced to the conclusion that I should have to do the job myself, but first I retained Old Nart's services in an advisory capacity.

He watched me begin, 'With geese you have to do three pluckings,' he warned.

This startled me. I went on plucking, the wing feathers, and then the breast. After I had done that fairly well I realized that the goose had not only an overcoat but also a waistcoat underneath. And that I should have to go over the carcass again and remove all the down. 'We call it doom,' said Old Nart. 'The doom is the devil.' By the time I had finished the second plucking, I was in full agreement.

'But what's the third plucking?' I asked.

Old Nart laughed and pointed to my clothes white with down and feathers. 'Pluck yourself!' he said.

*   *   *

After dark on Boxing Day it has long been Sam's custom to take a walk over the fields to Old Ben's farm.

Once again this year I could follow his progress in that direction by the flickering light of the old hurricane lantern that he always carried on these convivial occasions. I could imagine the two of them there, crouched over the log fire, rivalry forgotten, smoking their pipes and sipping Old Ben's famous parsnip wine.

Sam could leave without more than the usual anxiety inseparable from a farm. The pigs and the old mare, Honey, had been fed; the sows were snoring in the straw, and Judy had been milked. The only doubtful factor was Susie the young gilt, soon expecting her first litter of pigs. Even that problem has been entrusted to safe hands in Old Nart. That Worthy had already given his verdict. 'P'raps she will and p'raps she

won't,' he had said and promised to have another look before midnight.

So there was nothing much to worry about. They discussed the weather, the fact that all their fields were ploughed in good time, the way the drains were running, and the prospects for next harvest. The more wine Sam drank the better he felt those prospects would be.

This year Ben produced for Sam's inspection his Christmas present, a big green parrot in a wire cage that his nephew had brought him from overseas.

They kept talking till nearly midnight, at which hour (according to Old Ben) all kinds of strange ghosts walked the farm, including an old white sow with a clanking chain which Sam would probably meet on his way home. It reminded Sam about Susie. So, after having 'one for the mud' he took leave of a friendly host and set off back over the fields.

There was a dim light in the piggeries. A bearded figure stood there, leaning over Susie's sty. 'How is she?' gasped Sam.

'She's pigged,' said the old man. And, while Sam was vainly trying to count them, he added: 'Nine good pigs, a New Year present for you.'

Turkeys and Geese

DANIEL DEFOE

Writing in 1724 Defoe tells of the poultry prepared for the London Christmas market. In 1865 Suffolk and Norfolk still maintained the reputation for breeding more turkeys than anywhere else, as well as a prodigious number of geese. Whereas geese used to be 'shod', by driving them over cool tar or clay and then across sand to coat their webs, the birds are now transported by rail. In 1863 seventeen thousand geese and thirteen thousand turkeys arrived at the terminus in Shoreditch.

I can't omit, however little it may seem, that this county of Suffolk is particularly famous for furnishing the city of London and all the counties round, with turkeys; and that it is thought there are more turkeys bred in this county, and the part of Norfolk that adjoins to it, than in all the rest of England, especially for sale. Nor will it be found so inconsiderable an article as some may imagine, if this be true which I received an accurate account of from a person living on the place, (viz.) that they have counted 300 droves of turkeys (for they drive them all in droves on foot) pass in one season over Stratford Bridge on the River Stour, on the road from Ipswich to London. These droves, as they say, generally contain from three hundred to a thousand each drove; so that one may suppose them to contain 500 one with another, which is 150,000 in all; and yet this is one of the least passages, the

Turkeys and geese for sale in North Road, Ipswich, *c.* 1900

numbers which travel by New Market Heath, and the open country and the forest, and also by Sudbury and Clare, being many more.

For the further supplies of the markets of London with poultry, of which these counties particularly abound: they have within these few years found it practicable to make the geese travel on foot too, as well as the turkeys, and a prodigious number are brought up to London in droves from the farthest parts of Norfolk. They begin to drive them generally in August, by which time the harvest is almost over, and the geese may feed in the stubbles as they go. Thus they hold on to the end of October, when the roads begin to be too stiff and too deep for their broad feet and short legs to march in. Besides these methods of driving these creatures on foot, they have of late also invented a new method of carriage, being carts formed on purpose, with four stories or stages to put the creatures in one above another, by which invention one cart will carry a very great number and for the smoother going, they drive with two horses a-breast, like a coach, so quartering the road for the ease of the gentry that thus ride; changing horses they travel night and day; so that they bring the fowls, 70, 80 or 100 miles in two days and one night. The horses in this new-fashioned voiture go two a-breast, as above, but no perch below as in a coach, but they are fastened together by a piece of wood lying cross-wise upon their necks, by which they are kept even and together, and the driver sits on the top of the cart, like as in the public carriages for the army, etc. In this manner they hurry away the creatures alive, and infinite numbers are thus carried to London every year.

A Lowestoft Christmas

LOWESTOFT JOURNAL

Three men were killed and more than thirty injured in a railway accident at Barnby Siding, near Lowestoft, on Christmas Eve, 1891. Villagers hastened to the scene to give what help they could. One of the helpers, Mr Beamish, became known as 'The Giant of Barnby', a subject of much local folklore.

The disaster caused the utmost consternation amidst the inhabitants of Lowestoft and the neighbourhood generally, and

Lowestoft Bridge, 1890s

it will be many a day before the sad affair will be forgotten by those who were at all affected by it. . . .

Villagers hastened to the scene to give what help they could. Foremost among these was Mr Amos Beamish, a man of almost gigantic strength, which he turned to such good account as to make one almost believe it was especially increased for the occasion. . . . Amidst the cruel fog, which had been the prime cause of the disaster might be seen his massive form moving from place to place, here assisting one from a quantity of debris, and again with his axe cutting away some of the woodwork of the wrecked carriages and releasing the sufferers who had been literally imbedded in the wreck of the ill-fated train.

Fishing fleet at Lowestoft

Nativity Play at Hollesley Colony

BRENDAN BEHAN

Brendan Behan, the Irish playwright, was born in Dublin in 1923. At sixteen he was sent to the Borstal at Hollesley, a detention centre noted for its Suffolk Punch horses, which it breeds, works on the farm, and takes to agricultural shows.

In the last week of November our Matron asked fellows she met in the corridors to go down to the Library, where she was picking a cast for the Nativity Play for Christmas . . .

I was talking to Tom and to Ken Jones, and then the Matron called Ken over to her and told us he was going to act St Joseph.

Joe looked over at him and said, 'That there Kenneth – 'e shouldn't be St Joseph – e's a C. of E.'

'You silly born bastard,' said Charlie, 'we got St Joseph and Jesus Christ, the lot, in the C. of E. Church, same as you 'ave.'

The door opened, and Charlie whistled in a whisper.

'My, my,' said Joe, 'get on that.'

A girl of about nineteen had come in. Some of the blokes made room for her beside Matron.

'She's the wife of Mr Hackbell, the young screw over the farm machinery,' said a Welsh bloke behind us. He was on a tractor himself. 'She is going to act the Virgin Mary.'

'I'll be the Holy Ghost,' said Joe.

The Welshman looked away, shocked.

I looked away from him myself. Not that I was shocked, God knows, but I was afraid I should burst out laughing and that we would embarrass the girl, who was among a lot of strange blokes and Borstal boys, at that. You wouldn't mind Matron, she was a Borstal boy, herself, damn near, but it would be, also, letting her down before the girl.

'Come along, dear,' said Matron, 'we've only just begun.'

The blokes stood up and made way politely for her, and murmured 'Excuse me,' as she went to the place where Matron and Ken Jones stood.

'She's a smasher all right', said Joe.

'She is that,' said I.

Charlie looked at her and nodded and said: 'She's in the nativity play. She's the Virgin Mary.'

'I know,' said Joe, 'I wish I could be the Baby.'

Charlie said nothing, but looked away, and then Matron called us over to give the rest of us our parts.

Charlie and 538 Jones were shepherds, and 'Gordon-get-your-horse' was the head shepherd.

He was delighted over this, but he had to explain to Matron that he would have no lamb available at that time, but that he would have a little kid goat that he was rearing. It was a little undersized goat born out of its time, and it was so small now that it wouldn't be any bigger than a lamb at Christmas when we put on the play.

Matron said that that was great, and that he needn't bring this kid goat to rehearsals but only on the night of the play.

Chewlips and Jock and Tom Meadows were inn-keepers and census-takers. Joe and I were picked for two of the wise men, and the third wise man, the Black King, was a real black bloke, who played in our front row at Rugby. He was the bloke from Tiger Bay they called Christian.

'That's all for now,' said the Matron, 'you can go now, except for Kenneth Jones, and Taffy Lloyd.

Taffy Lloyd was a Welsh bloke that was singing a hymn in the play . . .

*   *   *

At Christmas we had the Nativity Play on Christmas Eve, the screws all brought their families to it; Matron told us she was very proud of us, and so did the Squire.

On Christmas Day we had a big dinner, with duff, and old 'Ucker put rough cider into it, which was very decent of him, even though the blokes said he had a bloody great barrel of it up in his house that was sent to him by his brother in Devon.

Christmas Chaos

JOHN WALLER

The Revd John Waller is Rector of Waldringfield, Henley and Newborne. He is the fifth generation of the Waller family to be rector of these parishes – an unbroken line from father to son for 143 years. Before he was ordained, John Waller was a North Sea trawlerman, sailing from Grimsby and was in the first cod war in 1959. In this piece he takes us behind the scenes of a nativity play at an unidentified parish.

Our Lord's birthday is celebrated every year with a re-enactment of the drama at Bethlehem which is performed in the chancel of the church by the Boys' Brigade and the Brownies. I never cease to marvel that this same story always has a fresh interpretation of this historical event.

There is always one rehearsal, and one only, to preserve the spontaneity of this theatrical piece. As usual it is more of a pantomime than a play. The shouting and bawling to maintain order in the vestry can be heard all over the village. The constant issuing of threats to quell further rioting can never be heard above the babel of a hundred different conversations going on at the same time. The choosing of the characters to represent the Holy Family are type cast if possible. The scruffy looking lads finish up as the shepherds and the dandy mumsy-wumsy boys are the kings. The girls always portray the heavenly host and always sing beautifully. Thus the stage is set for this unique event.

Sunday arrives and the church begins to fill to capacity. Grannies and Grampas and aged Aunts and Uncles, parents

Westleton church

and babes in arms are all there – line upon line, pew upon pew. All faces fixed on the chancel to see if they can recognize the member of their family who has suddenly been elevated to stardom.

The drama begins five minutes before the performance starts. A shepherd reports that Joseph, who was never enthralled with the Virgin Mary from the outset, had abandoned her and, making good his escape through the vestry window, was on his way home. Hastily, two 'heavies' were despatched to catch him up and remind him of his parental obligations. It was not long before the struggling Joseph was brought before me and I enquired of him the reason for his behaviour. Joseph complained bitterly that he never did fancy the Virgin Mary, but Joseph eventually agreed to remain Joseph.

The cradle was a crate marked 'Lemons from Israel' which seemed appropriate for the occasion.

The show began with the Virgin Mary and the reluctant Joseph taking up positions in the chancel. The Holy Family had hardly got seated when fighting broke out under the belfry between the shepherds and the wise men. Sceptres were being used as cudgels and crooks as spears. This was a real show-stopper. Brown Owl and Boys' Brigade officers struggled to keep the assailants apart and endeavoured to discover the cause of this affray. It came to light that a shepherd had called one of the glittering Eastern kings a 'poof'. The king retorted by calling the shepherd 'Fat Guts' – violence had then ensued. Peace and goodwill was finally established; the play continued . . . one of the angels had a collapsed wing which gave the impression of drunkeness, although she was obviously unaware of this.

The birthday scene proceeded more or less uneventfully – there were the usual forgotten lines and impromptu remarks which caused great hilarity in the audience, including that of

the Virgin Mary who was meant to say, 'Behold, I am the handmaid of the Lord,' and said instead, 'Behold, I am the landlord.'

In the final scene when the members of the cast dispersed to the vestry and the belfry, the front end of the ox turned right and the rear-end turned left and the animal was completely severed in two. It was a case of the front-end not knowing what the rear-end was doing. Thus ended yet another chaotic Holy Birthday celebration with all the accompanying joys and sorrows.

Carol Singers

ADRIAN BELL

The following scene is from the 1950s in Northgate, Beccles, where Adrian Bell went to live after retiring from farming.

Dreaming of the flowers of Christmas, listening to Scarlatti, enjoying the sight of my still butterfly-gay cyclamen blooms, I was interrupted by a ring of the front door bell, long and insistent. I dragged myself out of my comfortable chair and went to the door. There stood a small boy who looked like a young hedgehog. We faced each other in the glimmer from a street lamp, I having groped out of my reverie through the dark hall, feeling like Mole.

'Well,' I said.

'Carols,' he said.

'Haven't heard a sound,' I said.

'We bin singing,' he said.

'How many of you?'

'Three on us.'

I looked around, could only see one, but heard knockers being rat-tatted, bells being rung elsewhere.

'I never heard you,' I repeated.

'We bin singing,' he insisted.

'What?'

'Once in Royal David's City.'

'What else can you sing?'

'Once in Royal David's City.'

'Who was David?'

'He were a king.' (General knowledge or deduction from the epithet?)

'What was his city?'

Pause. 'Shall we sing it?'

'Go on.'

He called into the shadows, 'C'm arn!'

A second shock-headed little hedgehog-boy appeared. The chorus-leader produced a curled, dog-eared scrap of paper, and they began. The tune was recognizable, and the words. Verse one, two, three – they plugged away. At the end of the third verse their voices disappeared in a squeak and a fog on the high notes of,

'Christian children all must be . . .'

'All right,' I said. The third member of the choir had appeared in time for verse three. I gave them a sixpenny bit, wished them a merry Christmas and closed the door. Through its glass panel I saw them engaged in a wrestling match for the office of treasurer.

Carolling with Benjamin Britten and Peter Pears

BARBARA BROOK

*Barbara Brook was headmistress at Aldeburgh Primary
School from 1948 to 1955, and then a HM Inspector of
Schools. On retirement she returned to Aldeburgh where she
still lives. She was a founder member of the Aldeburgh Music
Club which started in 1951–2 with the active support of
Benjamin Britten and Peter Pears. Early meetings were held
at their home in Crabbe Street, Aldeburgh.*

Local instrumentalists and singers met to perform music in small
groups and for their own enjoyment. Trios, quartets, SATB or
other vocal combinations arranged to rehearse, and to perform at
the next club meeting. Although there were several skilled
recorder players, treble and tenor, the instrument was frowned
upon until Peter Pears 'took up' the bass recorder. It was an
intriguing sight, to say the least, to see him hastily consult the
fingering chart hanging from the music stand. But from then on
the recorder was accepted as a bona fide musical instrument – and
maintained 'true' pitch at least as adequately as some of the
violins in the ensembles in spite of the initial prophecies.

· *A Suffolk Christmas* ·

The annual carol service at Bury St Edmunds Cathedral which
is lit entirely by candles and accompanied by an all-male choir
(*East Anglian Daily Times*)

65

In December 1952 a group of us went carol singing with Benjamin Britten and Peter Pears. On the second evening we decided to finish the programme at the Margaret Ogilvie Almshouses near Aldringham Church, some two miles from Aldeburgh. We stood alongside the fence, the terrace of cottages indistinct in the darkness. (I discovered afterwards that only the kitchen entrances faced the fence). One elderly man stood by a small building, listening to our carolling. At the finish, he took his pipe from his mouth, and said: 'Arr, very noice, tew. Yar singin' t' the pump house.'

We retired with subdued mirth.

The Garden

DOREEN WALLACE

Doreen Wallace was the author of over thirty novels, most of them set in Suffolk. But she also wrote a month-by-month account (In a Green Shade, 1950), *of her garden at Wortham Manor.*

My year has turned, in mild, dark weather, and I am thankful for no gale warnings for shipping. The wireless tells us that there have only been seven white Christmases this century, in the southern part of the country. I doubt if there ever were all those white Christmasses which figure in our grandmothers' tales: the old saw that when days grow longer, cold comes stronger, seems to contradict the pretty figments which we would prefer to

believe. For the arable farmer, the white Christmas is no blessing – he still has sugar-beet in heaps along the roadside, if not actually in the ground. Snow harms the beet to the extent of weakening the sugar-content, while frost ruins it altogether. And you never yet found the farmer who protected his beet properly, or indeed anything else. When it is too late, when the damage has been done, the farm-hands will run around with coverings of straw or beet-tops, just as at harvest-time, when the machines are actually needed, they are being hustled off to the blacksmith for repairs, and when the corn is being stacked it is after the thunderstorm that the stack-cloth is remembered.

There seems to be a lot about weather in this book. For the country person the weather is a constant companion; like a husband, it is sometimes friend, sometimes enemy, but always there. And whereas in extremity one can divorce a husband, one cannot divorce the weather. Till death us do part, I am committed to obedience to this incalculable temperament.

How it rules me! So many of my occupations, and almost all my pleasures, take place out of doors that a whole week's plans may have to be cancelled, urgent work put off indefinitely, and pleasure simply wiped out, because of vagaries up aloft. Townspeople are far less conscious of weather. It enters so rarely into their plans that they arrange their lives independently of it, often only becoming conscious that there is any weather while waiting for a bus. But of course when their annual holiday looms up, it is a different story; the weather is their master then, while we countryfolk, who have learned to be opportunists all the year round and who seldom have a stated holiday, can afford to be philosophical about it.

This is a mother-of-pearl day, the sky covered with soft grey clouds whose sunward edges gleam silver here and there. The air is mild, and there is no breath of wind. It would pass for a summer day in my inclement north. The birds, misled by the warmth, keep murmuring springlike songs, and the yellow jasmine is lightly starred with flowers.

Christmas Eve 1938

PETER GERRELL

Peter Gerrell was born in Reydon in 1932 of a family that had lived in the parish for over three hundred years. The Reydon village sign was designed by him.

I've always thought that a cluster of holly sprigs bound together makes the most attractive Christmas Tree. Their dark

green leaves hold the firelight to reflect droplets of golden rain into every corner. Even the getting was a joy, well worth wrapping up against the chill and bracing oneself to face the crisp December air and venture forth in Father's footsteps to the nearest tangled hedgerow. It was an event to be savoured.

Yet another Christmas ritual was making ready Mother's pantry to receive the annual influx of expected goodies. Mouth-watering morsels that would soon be jumping out of our old black oven and demanding lodging space until the great day. And what a scrumptious collection too. Gingerbreads, mince pies, shortcakes, sausage rolls, cheese straws and dozens more to titillate the taste buds when the time was right.

Of course the pinnacle of anticipation came with the ritual hanging of the stockings. Even though I'd long been mindful of where my little gifts came from and the sweat of whose brow made it possible, all of us played the Father Christmas role to its happy conclusion.

I heard Dad's boots crunching up the path. Old Gyp, I knew, would be scurrying somewhere behind him. Quickly jumping out of bed I thawed a peep-hole with the warmth of my hand on the window. Shadows were dancing about in the yard below. Caught in ripples of yellow lantern light the white underbelly of a plump rabbit flashed momentarily – a happy conclusion to Dad's supper walk with the old dog. Our traditional Boxing Day pie was safe for another year.

I noticed that the topmost logs in the yard woodpile sparkled with the breath of frost. Then as Father raised the lantern to hang by a nail on a linen post, a fluorescent tide of light swilled across the garden to uncover a countryside glistening with the work of old Jack. It seemed he hadn't confined his attention to our logpile.

Much later I was awakened by the familiar creaking of our gate protesting on its rusty hinges. Suddenly the back door

burst open and old Gyp was bounding and barking joyously down the path. An explosion of voices on the threshold signalled that Aunt Nellie had arrived, happy and laughing at the end of her annual Christmas Eve pilgrimage from old Bridge House. We always looked forward to her coming. She was a dear soul for whom Christmas held its true message.

There was no need for me to desert my warm bed for cold lino to discover what she was carrying. The ritual had already confined her to a bottle of Grandad's best parsnip wine and two dozen sausage rolls wrapped piping hot in two yards of oven cloth. I knew also that a ring of chairs would be drawn round the fire below and the offerings sampled while old times were mulled over. Father, in particular, would enjoy his dram of Grandad's 'fit for a king' parsnip wine, sitting in the shadows with firelight picking out the lines on his tired face. He knew

Friston after a heavy fall of snow in 1987

few such moments, hard work and the worry of finding it had etched the passing of yet untrodden years in his grey eyes. This blessed Christmas Eve custom was a pearl of joy in a year strung with strife.

The sound of laughter filtered through the house to gladden the night. Soon there was singing, as I knew there would be, 'Silent Night' followed by Nell's favourite, 'The Holly and the Ivy'. Glasses tinkled – chipped hand cups in reality and old Gyp barked once. A sure sign he'd been given a morsel of Aunt Nell's Christmas fare. A sausage roll no doubt.

The stairs creaked and heads appeared round my bedroom door. Whisperings filled the room. Aunt Nellie had arrived, finger to lips, no noise, for she'd heard reindeer overhead! Just time enough though to enjoy a sip of Grandad's wine. I caught my breath, my inside flew afire . . . Mother laughed. My sister in the other room wouldn't though. She always gulped down everything. I'd listen for the results of that! Now a sausage roll, crumbs on the pillow, crumbs in bed. A last goodnight kiss and as she stoops a tiny coloured blob is placed on my pillow. I know exactly what it is – I always did – a sugar mouse. Another part of the wonderful ritual.

All is still outside. The world is wrapped in a cottonwool cloak of silver moonlight. As far as the eye can see nothing stirs to fracture the magic of Christmas Eve. Jack Frost has transformed my little peep-hole into a magnificent lace-like web.

Suddenly a dog barks, to be answered by another in the far distance. Below a door slams and the night is once again alive to the sound of voices. 'Good Night' and 'Merry Christmas' fall from happy lips. The crunch of feet down the frozen path as hinges protest but squeak in vain as Father holds open the gate for our dear departing guest. Mother, I know, will be blowing kisses from the doorstep and waving her goodbyes until the last faint footfall.

All over the village now folk are spilling out into the night. Christmas Eve visiting is drawing to a close. Soon the midnight bells will herald Christmas Day and all mankind shall be at peace with the breath of it.

Familiar voices ring out everywhere. 'Good Night' our neighbour shouts across the garden, 'Merry Christmas to you all!' But he will, I know, call in for one quick glass to toast the best of friends.

'And a Merry Christmas to you too!' echoes my father's voice.

And that was the last I can remember of Christmas Eve 1938. But there would be no more like it – ever again!

Party Bells

ANNA HADFIELD

The late Anna Hadfield lived for twenty years at Barham Manor, the setting for this episode in 1964, which was graced by a pair of peafowl, the subject of her book A Peacock on the Lawn. *She was married to John Hadfield, the distinguished anthologist, and her book is a delight, as is that of her husband,* Love on a Branch Line, *also set in Suffolk.*

Last Christmas was a particularly gay and happy one. Jeremy and Maureen and our two grandsons, Heywood and Patrick, were due to arrive on Christmas Eve, so we had set up and decorated the Christmas tree the day before. We have the tree

THE YULE LOG

in the Garden Room, as there is plenty of space there for the children to play without knocking a decoration off the tree every few minutes. All our presents are put in individual heaps on a bed of pine branches round the tree.

When the family arrived about six o'clock nearly everything was organized. I say 'nearly everything' advisedly, as I remember I had a pile of gifts in my closet waiting to be wrapped and labelled later in the evening. But a meal was prepared, and wood fires were roaring in the big open hearths, and reflections of the flames were dancing on the red berries of the holly and the dark green leaves of the ivy with which we had decorated the rooms. The whole scene, in fact, was almost

73

unbelievably in accordance with the convention of the Victorian Christmas card.

The two little boys were, of course, in a state of great excitement. Not only was there the ritual hanging-up of the Christmas stocking for them to look forward to, but they were to stay up to an early dinner. After dinner we were expecting one of the most significant event of our Christmas – the arrival of the village choir to play carols on handbells.

Somewhere there may exist better handbell ringers than ours – although I have yet to hear them – but there can be no ringers alive who put more enthusiasm into their ringing or produce a more joyous sound. The choir consists of about twelve people of both sexes and of all ages, from youngsters of about nine years old to married couples.

On arrival they ring one carol outside our front door, gathered round a large lantern. It is a rigid convention that we all stay seated – and silent – inside the house until the first carol is ended. But it is much easier for them to see the music clearly if they come inside the house, and it is much more fun for us if we can see them ringing. So after this first carol they all come inside and troop through into the Garden Room.

Last Christmas Eve we were a particularly receptive audience. The Grampions had come round to listen to the carols with us, and so had our great friends and nearest neighbours, Hugh and Juliet Edwards. They have now, alas, moved out of Suffolk, and the knowledge that this was the last Christmas they would be with us lent poignancy to the evening. We managed to find chairs for the grown-ups. The two boys ready for bed and clad in pyjamas and dressing-gowns, squatted on the floor.

Heywood and Patrick had not heard the bell-ringers before. They sat absolutely still, for once, lost in wonder, while the choir played us all the old favourites from '*In Dulce Jubilo*' to '*While Shepherds Watched*'. I was torn between the pleasure of watching my grandsons and enjoying the look of fierce concentration and determination on the faces of some of the younger ringers.

The choir seemed to enjoy ringing the handbells as much as we enjoyed listening. But when they had finished 'Come All Ye Faithful' I thought the youngest ringer looked a little tired, so I suggested a break for refreshments.

We had prepared for this break as far as possible beforehand. We had orangeade for the youngest, and then we advanced through Pepsi Cola to beer, sherry or whisky for the older members. Everyone sat on the floor. While we passed round the drinks, Heywood and Patrick offered Christmas cake and mince pies, putting the plates on the floor while they examined the handbells, giving them a good shake with considerably less success than their owners. Some of the younger members of the choir are always shy at first, but this does not last long, and they are soon chatting away as fast as mouthfuls of plum cake will let them.

When all have eaten and drunk their fill the choir staggers to its feet. During this operation some of the younger ones invariably knock their glasses over and their faces turn a bright scarlet. We pretend not to notice.

John then hands over our gift of money – it usually goes for repairs to the church roof – to the oldest member of the choir, and he makes a short speech thanking them for the entertainment. At this point they always insist on ringing one more carol for us. How some of the children can manage this energetic exercise after all they have eaten and drunk amazes me.

As a finale the choir played for us 'Hark The Herald Angels Sing' and then they filed out, amidst a chorus of conventional sentiments, giggles and remarks upon the excellence of the cake. Our two little grandsons, by now thoroughly overexcited, were with difficulty prevented from following them

The Middleton Brass Band

down the drive. However, we reminded them that they had to hang up their stockings, so they went upstairs with their mother, and we promised to go up and say 'good-night' to them later.

We were left to have a quiet drink with our friends. So powerful is the spirit of Christmas – gently aided, of course, by another sort of spirit – that we were able to sit and contemplate with equanimity a floor littered with crumbs, a pool of orangeade, and the shattered fragments of two of my best wine glasses.

Yuletide at Debenham Vicarage

JAMES CORNISH

James Cornish, who was born at the vicarage in Debenham in 1860, was the son of the Revd Charles Cornish, vicar of Debenham from 1860 to 1883. One night when it was snowing, the Revd Charles Cornish came home without his greatcoat. When asked by his wife what he had done with it, he explained that he had met a parishioner: 'He had such a thin suit and it was white with snow, so I gave him my coat.' Many years later James Cornish met the parishioner who showed him the coat, then more green than black. The parishioner said: 'It has got thin now, but if it don't allus warm the body it never fail to warm the heart.'

Christmas was the time when our father and mother gave their two parties for people of the parish, the children and the old folk. Vaughan's birthday was 22 December, and the Christmas tree was decorated for his birthday party. The whole of the process was watched and carried out by us with the keenest interest. A few rather mean spruce firs grew in the vicarage garden, and one of them was felled and the top utilized. To see the gardener, 'nelus Last, swinging his axe against the tree till it tottered and fell was delightful. Then came the planting of the top in the

This Debenham butcher still cures bacon and ham in the traditional Suffolk manner

'cinder hod', when we could help to stamp the soil down to 'firm it in'. Next the decorating of the tree with glass balls and crackers, and the fixing of holders for the tapers. The invitations were sent by hand to the children of tradesmen and others in the place who were about the same age as ourselves, and since the gardener was 'no scholar', he was told the names of those invited, and the letters were arranged according to the order in which the respective homes would come on his way down the street. These he would place in different pockets of his coat and long-sleeved waistcoat and carry four between the fingers of his left hand. 'Let me see, Madam, first is for Mr Frank Gooding, next Mr Emerson, next Mr Simpson', and so on till he reached the further end of the street. Perhaps he would need to make a second journey if the invitations outnumbered his pockets and fingers, but he made no mistakes.

It used to be a delightful evening; tea was in the big dining-room with the tree still unlit at the end of it; later the lighting of the tree and the giving of presents. Let us remember that probably not one of our guests saw any Christmas tree except ours, and thus we can understand their delight in the brightness of the tapers, the reflections from the ornaments and the presents they received.

The second entertainment my father called his only dinner party of the year. After morning service on Christmas Day, about twenty of the older men and women in Debenham were invited to come to the vicarage, and there would be ready for them a great round of prime beef, rolled ribs. Not one of them was likely to have tasted such a joint since the previous Christmas Day. When all had assembled they took their places, the men on one side and the women on the other, not because it was so ordered, but because of 'the custom'. At the foot of the table sat the Parish Clerk by right of his office, not of his age, and he said 'grace before dinner'. The giving of thanks afterwards was assigned to Mr Cullum, Senior Deacon of the Chapel, for the invitations were not limited to church people. Mr Cullum was more lengthy in his grace than Theobald the Clerk, and always added a clause invoking blessings on 'All who are beneath this ruff'. He took his office seriously, and one day said to my father, 'We two be both shepherds.'

The vicar carved, and his question to each person was, 'Do you like it home-done or rare?', the Suffolk for well-browned or reddish slices. We waited on the old people and poured out the beer. Plum pudding followed: the men like two helpings of beef and one of pudding; the women, one of the former and two of the latter. Then we had our dinner in the drawing-room and afterwards went back to relight the Christmas tree, for the tapers had been extinguished at the children's party before they had burned out. The old folk, especially the women, delighted in the sparkle of the lighted tree almost as much as the children did.

The long table was then reduced to its normal size and all gathered round the fire. Cups of tea were brought in before the light of the short winter's day was gone, and the aged guests left before it was too dark for them to make their way home easily.

Christmas 1898

HENRY RIDER HAGGARD

Henry Rider Haggard, the novelist, was also a gentleman farmer at Ditchingham. He went to a farm in 1889 in Norfolk, just over the Suffolk border and close to Bungay. He also had a house at Kessingland, Suffolk.
The extracts here are from entries in A Farmer's Year, *his commonplace-book for 1898.*

Christmas Day
. . .Yesterday, as the frost continued, we were obliged to give up the ploughing and take to the carting of manure. While I was walking along a hedgerow I saw a sight that I have never seen before. Suddenly, about fifty yards ahead of me, a cock pheasant sprang from the fence and lit upon the ground with an angry crow, flicking up one wing in a very curious fashion. Next second I learned the reason, for after him came a medium-sized black and white cat, which evidently had tried to pounce upon him in the hedge. On seeing him the pheasant took to his legs and the disappointed cat slunk back to shelter.

I did not know before that a cat would attack so powerful a bird.

Royal Duke, the prize ox, made his last appearance at Ditchingham this evening in the shape of sirloin of beef. The meeting was painful to me who had known him from a calf, but I must admit that he was excellent eating. Oh! what carnivores we are!

Yesterday the frost broke, with the result that this Christmas has not the beauty of that of last year, the weather being dull and mild, towards nightfall softening into rain. In the afternoon I went to hear some carols sung in the neighbouring church of Broome. Afterwards, a friend of mine who lives there, gave me some curious facts illustrative of the decrease of population in that parish. It is his habit to make a present of meat at Christmas to every cottage inhabitant of Broome, and he informed me that the difference in its cost owing to the shrinkage of population between this year and last is something really remarkable.

27 December

Today a fierce gale is blowing from the sou'-west, and against it, – having business there – I struggled to Kessingland, accomplishing most of the journey upon a bicycle. The ride from Lowestoft, in the very teeth of the wind, was the hardest I have ever undertaken. Very frequently, indeed, I was obliged to dismount and push behind, a duty that was not made more entertaining by the vision of a curate, cigarette in mouth, sailing past me in the opposite direction, his feet reposing on the rests. I wonder why it is, by the way, that most curates and many clergymen ride bicycles so madly? Thrice have I nearly fallen a victim to their rage – the last time, indeed, I just escaped being run down by a coasting covey of six of them at once.

At length I turned down the lane which leads to Cliff

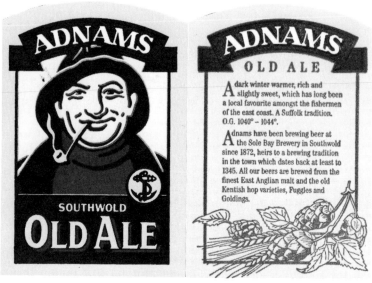

A dark winter warmer, rich and slightly sweet, a favourite
among fishermen on the east coast

Grange, the very easternmost dwelling, I suppose, in the
whole kingdom, and as the wind was now upon my side, got
along much better, until a sudden and ferocious gust blew me
and the bicycle several yards into a ploughed field. The sight
from the cliff was very grand – a sullen, tempest fretted sea
raging beneath a low, and sullen sky. But a gale from the
sou'-west is not that which does damage on the eastern coat –
it is the nor'-easter that we dread, especially if it be
accompanied by very high tides. This is what happened in the
great storm of last December, when the tide and the sea rose
higher than they are believed to have done for the best part of a
century. The damage at Lowestoft, Southwold, Pakefield,
etc., was enormous, and as I had recently come into possession
of this Kessingland property, my state of mind until I heard
that it had taken no harm can be imagined.

A Woman's Point of View

EAST ANGLIAN DAILY TIMES

Lady Stradbroke thinks that the real joy of Christmas is in having the family at home because it is so essentially a children's time. It is the presence of small children in the home which makes the celebration of Christmas so much more worth-while.

Not only is it a time to look forward to for the fun of the decorations, the presents and carols; the good food and the parties, but also for the feeling of goodwill towards mankind and the kindness and cheerfulness which prevail everywhere.

It is an important time too because it is the only season of the year when everyone (even if they never enter a church at any other time) makes an effort to go to a service, persuading many of their friends and members of their household to go too.

Lady Mears, who as Margaret Tempest, is known and loved the whole world over for her wonderful illustrations in the Little Grey Rabbit books writes of the happy memories she has of the perfect Christmases of her childhood. Her message will remind many of what seems in retrospect a gentler and more gracious time than the one in which we live now.

'The Christmases of my childhood seem to me to be perfect. To everyone in the house the important thing was the meaning

83

of Christmas – the birth of the Christ-child. Everybody was a little nicer to everybody else.

'There was the anticipation and the excitement; the decorations and the arrival of the postman. The present tables were filled with toys, and there was a pile of new books, including always a bound volume of *Sundays*, looked forward to and seized upon at once by me.

'There were the usual good things to eat and drink; the warmth and the lights, the laughter and fun.

'All were enhanced by the Christmas hymns, at church in the morning and round the piano in the evening, which brought peace and joy to the heart of a child.

'There was too, a slight feeling of awe at the sound of the church bells and the voices of the carol singers which came through the night. It was a holy time.

'The ideal thing is to have a house full of children for Christmas, or to give some happiness to children who for some reason would have a poor or neglected Christmas; or to someone old and lonely or forgotten. If one can do this, one will without doubt have a happy Christmas oneself.'

Mrs Florence Evans is the headmistress of Needham Market Primary School and the wife of George Ewart Evans, the well-known writer and broadcaster.

'For me it's the peacefulness of Christmas Day that matters most. The weeks before Christmas are frenzied, breaking-up festivities at school, the arrival of the family from school and college, last minute shopping, the stocking of the larder to meet all emergencies – and, then suddenly, on Christmas Eve, peace descends, heralded by the voices of carol singers, mysterious in the country darkness.

'Christmas has a special "feel" about it. There's no hurry, no sense of urgency. Everybody helps with household chores. Preparing the dinner, the major occupation of the morning, is a pleasant task. We have the traditional Christmas dinner at midday, so that the rest of the day may be left free for whatever activity individual members of the family may choose.

'My husband and I retreat to easy chairs by a blazing fire and, as dusk gathers, talk or read. My favourite Christmas book is still Beatrix Potter's *Tailor of Gloucester*. I knew it as a child, but my husband, who was introduced to it for the first time when the children were young, finds it as delightful as I do. I suppose it's rather silly for two middle-aged people to renew their acquaintance with Simpkin, year after year, but he's as much part of Christmas as the holly and the evergreens that decorate our old house.

'Tea is always a ceremonial occasion. The girls decorate the table and call us in when everything is ready. I remember seeing the candlelight reflected in my eldest daughter's eyes as she sat in a high chair at her first Christmas tea twenty-one years ago. I shall look for the reflected light in four pairs of eyes this year.

'I have not mentioned Christmas cards or presents. This side of Christmas has become more commercialized that I've developed a kind of "sales resistance" during the last few years. Of course there will be presents and cards, but they don't seem relevant to my "ideal" Christmas.'

How does the business woman like to spend her Christmas and what is her attitude to all the frenzied preparations which now mark our observation of the birth of Christ.

Miss Beaumont of Felixstowe who is the only woman to occupy a managerial post in one of Marks & Spencers stores gives a contribution full of homely detail.

'As one of what is nowadays considered to be a large family, the youngest of six, all my life Christmas has meant the traditional family gathering. A family Christmas – the annual gathering of young and old and in betweens with all the hectic planning of food, preparation of meals and washing-up, which is all part of the excitement and warm feeling of security brought about by a family Christmas.

'And as to this Christmas. Being a business woman, with many and varied responsibilities, for me it is a culmination of careful detailed organization covering every aspect. It involves continuous checking and supervision to ensure that the result aimed at is in fact achieved.

'As Christmas approaches, so the pace accelerates and it is indeed very near Christmas before I can settle down to consider my own personal plans and thoughts.

'I feel I need time for the "unwinding" process before complete relaxation, before I can really appreciate not only the good things to eat and drink, but also to realize and remember

yet once again the true spirit and meaning of the Festival of Goodwill and Peace. Without that understanding Christmas is empty.

As you ask me how, if I had complete freedom of choice, I would spend the perfect Christmas, I can only say I would love to spend it as I have spent so many Christmases during my life – with my family – hectic work and all.'

Mrs David Black, the wife of a well-known Suffolk farmer, gives a glimpse of what makes the perfect Christmas for a young mother.

Christmas to her is a ritual which must always be the same as far as possible. Home to Mother's, with turkey for midday dinner and the washing-up done in time for the Queen's speech.

All being well, this Christmas Day will follow the usual pattern, but this time it will be shared, (perhaps without obvious appreciation) by a daughter of six months as well as by the two-year-old Elizabeth.

Mrs Black is looking forward to recapturing the magic of Christmas because Elizabeth is now old enough to enjoy her stocking and all the other traditional delights. She hopes to get as much pleasure out of 'Oh look what Father Christmas has brought me' as Elizabeth, and I am sure she will.

Pleasures after the children are in bed, will be simple ones: listening to the gramophone, roasting chestnuts, playing games, preferably pencil and paper ones as it is a welcome change to sit down.

Christmas Candles 1939

ADRIAN BELL

Not long before the outbreak of war in 1939, Adrian Bell and his family went to live at Redisham. This extract is from Apple Acre.

I have a demi-john of cider left, old, deep as sunset. I had it from a friend who has a hundred acres and a mill and a cider press on the Suffolk border. He grinds his own corn in the mill, and makes his own cider in the press. He and his wife can never drink all he makes before another brew is ready; so it gets older and older.

I go to seek it in my cellar, for this is Christmas Eve. I pass three withered arthritic-looking legs sitting on the stairs. They are stuffed with little presents. Nora creeps into the children's room and fastens them in place.

Anthea is the presiding genius of this Christmas. Father Christmas is instinctively comprehended (after all what more credible than a jolly old man distributing toys all round?). Moreover, she has seen him, as she will tell you. It is true: I saw him myself. In the town market square, while a small, glittering snow sifted down, he came in a cart drawn by what looked like a reindeer – (At least it had reindeer's antlers. They reminded me of a pair on our doctor's wall: Father Christmas had much his figure) – followed by children singing carols, flanked by swinging lanterns, round and round the great Christmas tree standing in the square. Snow on the roofs all round, and old windows glowing. There was a spirit abroad that night; something lovely that had lived in this land raised its head. But the children departed, and traffic flowed again and white headlamps broke through. Still, after that who could doubt? I did not even myself. That was the last Christmas before war.

The twins are not old enough yet to understand about Father Christmas. Not for want of Anthea telling. Loudly telling.

Christmas had become a feverish effort to boost up trade, those last years. Its lovely spirit was lost with commercial Father Christmases standing in muddy gutters. Trust money-making to pick up a bit of old legend and put it in the cash register. Christmas morning came to have a relapsed feeling, a thank-God-the-shopping's-over feeling, a view of shuttered shops in the mind's eye.

And now. Yesterday afternoon I sat and listened to the singing of carols from King's College Chapel. I saw in my mind again that building which I can never approach without being filled with a sense of life. And the singing was like the foundation-stone of a new England.

This morning I go to drink the health of some friends. The children are absorbed in their stocking presents (though still Martin's old rag doll is the favourite plaything), Nora in the preparation of the Christmas dinner. I explain to the lady of the house when I go that the hour of our drinking together here is the most critical in the cooking of the dinner, so Nora could not come. I find myself deep in conversation to right and left, till I notice that people are thinning out, and take my leave. I am in that careless mood in which one reaches for the first coat one sees and has forgotten the way out. As I cycle off I recollect the acceptance of an invitation from my host to go on the river with him in his boat and fish. As I know nothing of fishing there seems something a little curious about it, it being winter. Perhaps we are to sit wrapped in old coats waiting for pike.

The cockerel I killed for Christmas weighed $7\frac{1}{4}$ lbs., and along with home-cured Bath chap, sausages, stuffing, and that old cider of Suffolk, makes a glorious meal. The plum pudding is good too; but not quite equal to one we ate last year which was two years old. My friends of the morning are having a goose from the farm opposite their house. There were a dozen of these geese, and it was a pleasant sight to see them walking out every morning in single file. As Christmas approached the procession dwindled till there were only two left. Then one. Every morning they saw the goose destined for their own table walk out alone. And now they are eating it – a little sadly.

An American's Wartime Christmas

ROBERT ARBIB

Robert Arbib was an American serviceman stationed in Suffolk during the Second World War. Later he was in the campaigns in Normandy and Brittany. His memories of Suffolk are contained in Here We are Together *written in 1945, far from Suffolk where he said 'we were close to the Heart of England'.*

· A Suffolk Christmas ·

Christmas is a quiet, family, churching day at Sudbury, a day to be spent at home, in visiting friends, and in walks about the countryside. But Christmas evening and Boxing Day – the day following Christmas – are the times for feasts and revelry in Sudbury, as they are in all England.

I got quietly and happily unsober on Christmas night in Sudbury, in keeping with the prevelant spirit of the town, which was not one of strict sobriety. It started at Daphne's house, where we had had a big Christmas dinner and had fallen asleep in chairs around the fire, passing a wet, cheerless afternoon, in quiet comfort. Later in the afternoon we had some tea, with whisky to go with it. And then some more tea and more whisky.

Then we went next door to The Half Moon, and went in the back door, because Daphne's friend, Phyllis, was the publican's daughter. We sat in the back room of The Half Moon drinking ales and 'gin and bitters' and playing with Phyllis's handsome son, Rodney. Phyllis had given him a box of cardboard coloured squares and discs for Christmas, and I thought it was high time that Rodney, aged two, should be able to tell red from yellow and green. But it evidently wasn't.

We sat around the back room, Daphne and Daphne's mother and Phyllis, whose husband was in the Middle East, and Phyllis's father and mother and Rodney. And presently others came – Doreen and her sister from across the street, and a young man I never saw again, and presently, old George. Old George was eighty, a big, bluff, ruddy man, and his old pewter mug was filled with a pint of dark. He sat by the fire, leaning on his cane, and never said a word.

Daphne kissed him good evening, which he liked, and his eyes followed the blonde girl wherever she went. When he felt like a sip of the beer, he would nod at the mug, and Daphne would hand it to him from the table, and he would drink, and hand the mug back to Daphne. Doreen played a few songs on

the old piano in the corner, and we sang. Phyllis's father got out the bottles of whisky he had been saving for Christmas and we had drinks all round. Then each of us bought another round of drinks and we laughed a lot about the sprig of mistletoe under the doorway.

Presently Rodney was put to bed, and Daphne and Phyllis and I stepped out into the rainy black night, and went down to The Royal Oak to see who was about. But first we stopped at The Christopher and had a 'bitter', and then we stopped at The Bear and said hello to everyone and played a pin-ball machine. And then we went on to The Royal Oak.

The Oak, as it was popularly called, was an old oak-beamed low-ceilinged pub with tiny rooms, but it was always popular, crowded, and considered one of the better-class pubs in Sudbury. . . . To-night it was jammed, and noisy, and clouded with blue smoke, and decorated with evergreen and holly. Everyone was talking, shouting, laughing, singing; you need not know anyone or introduce yourself or feel strange in The Oak on Christmas night, for once you stepped into the room a drink was thrust into your hand, and you were in a room full of friends. Each one tried to out-shout, out-laugh, and out-drink the other.

We met Clem here – a local merchant, and he joined our threesome with an armful of glasses. The smoke thickened, the noise and the heat increased, and the whole room spun about. Outside it was black, wet, chill, but there were occasional sounds of singing from the street. Sudbury was having a ruddy good Christmas. Only the observers on the rooftops faced the mist and listened with sober, thoughtful, keening ears and eyes. There had been an alert earlier in the day – the bombs had dropped somewhere in East Anglia, as they did almost every day, but to-night all was quiet – above.

It was inside these islands of good cheer – the little cells of life and excitement and fellowship – at The Royal Oak and

The Bear, The Black Boy and The Red Cow, The Anchor and The Railway Bell, and The Waggon and Horses, Half Moon, Four Swans, Christopher, Green Dragon, and The British Volunteer – in the public houses – that the common folk of Sudbury forgot the war and got royally drunk on Christmas night.

'Time, please, Gentlemen!' the publican shouted at 10 o'clock. We fumbled with the blackout curtains, shouted boisterous greetings and partings at everyone, kissed all the girls and women in the room, and then plunged out into the pitch inky envelope of night. 'Are you there, Daphne?'

'Here I am, over here. Strike a light.' And we danced, arm in arm, down the narrow Sudbury streets, bumping into poles, walls, people, doorways, stumbling over kerbs. 'Merry Christmas, everyone! Merry Christmas!'

Entertaining POWs

ANNE WOLRIDGE GORDON

Peter Howard bought Hill Farm, Brent Eleigh, in 1939 for £10 an acre. When the German prisoners-of-war came to work on the farm, they spoke little English and the Howard children were frightened of them. 'Germans were enemies' . . .

By the end of 1944, Willi and Rudi had become a part of the family. It was a firm friendship. The war mercifully seemed to be drawing to its close. It looked as if German prisoners might

soon be returning home. Howard wrote to the War Office and asked if Willi and Rudi could be invited to spend Christmas Day at Hill Farm. It was an unprecedented request. After long delays the permission was granted.

For the Howard family it was the last Christmas they would celebrate together for two years. The preparations were exciting. Warm balaclavas and socks were knitted for Willi and Rudi, the tree was decorated with red apples in the German style, and the children learnt the words of '*Stille Nacht*' ('Silent Night'). All the farm men and their wives were invited in, and the land girls came, the neighbours and all those whom the Howards had known during the war years.

The amazement on Willi and Rudi's faces as they stepped into the warm farm drawing-room was always to be remembered. It was hard for them to believe it was not some dream as

they sat awkwardly at the table eating off china and silver, which they had long since forgotten. After dinner they sat by the tree and wrote their first letters home to their families in East Germany. Then they unwrapped their gifts, and listened to the carols. Slowly they began to sing in German, it was the first time the children had seen grown men weep.

A Vet's Christmas Day

PHILIP RYDER-DAVIES

Philip Ryder-Davies is a Welshman who has practised as a veterinary surgeon in the Woodbridge district for the last fifteen years. He lives at Wickham Market where he has Suffolk Punches, Red Polls, a very large Suffolk ram and several breeds of rare poultry. He is also secretary to the Suffolk Horse Society and the Red Poll Cattle Society. Despite this he describes himself as a Welsh missionary rather than a Suffolk convert. He is much given to laughter but not, I think, on this particular Christmas Day.

I love Christmas. I love the preparations for it – the holly, the Christmas tree and the curious sense of impending pleasure that the festival induces.

Everything has to be the same each year; every detail of the

· A Suffolk Christmas ·

Christmas dinner in particular, must not change, so that the turkey is stuffed with thyme and parsley and accompanied by roast potatoes, mashed swede, Brussels sprouts cooked so that they are still crunchy, bread sauce, all to be followed by Christmas pudding accompanied by brandy butter and white sauce.

The day itself is very special. As I see to the needs of my Suffolk horses and Red Poll cattle, it really is a little difficult not to be reminded of that stable scene enacted so many years before and which the festival commemorates, then back into the house where the log fire has been lit early in the morning, which is something that the business of the rest of the year would never allow, and the day is spent with my family addressing the turkey or sitting reading the books that invariably arrive as presents.

For those of us whose jobs mean that we have to work at Christmas, this idyllic state of affairs can very easily be ruined. Having said that, after several years one becomes curiously stoical about this sort of thing and we end up just considering it as part of one's life. For many years I had in fact been able to enjoy Christmas Day in the bosom of my family, through, I

thought, the very generous nature of my partner, Dick Smith, who each year kindly offered to work on Christmas Day so that I could enjoy its pleasures and then I would work on Boxing Day. Looking back it is rather worrying to realize how long it took me to appreciate that no-one ever calls the 'vet' out on Christmas Day unless they are in dire straits and they always wait until Boxing Day, when all hell is let loose, and the first words each animal owner utters are to the effect that they couldn't possibly call you out on Christmas Day.

Several years ago, however, something had gone either right or wrong with the whole scheme, according to one's viewpoint, and I found myself on duty on Christmas Day. The day set off well enough without so much as a trill from the dreaded telephone until 12 noon, when it rang with depressing shrillness just as the smells from the turkey were starting to waft through the house. It was the cowman at a farm in the village of Easton, who said he had two cows in a bit of a muddle and could I get along there as soon as possible. A peculiarity of the Suffolk language is that nothing is exaggerated in any shape or form: 'We had some little bit of snow last night' means that there was a raging blizzard with six feet drifts and 'A bit of a muddle' will cover a fairly major drama. For a Welshman like myself, this can be difficult, as we magnify everything to make a decent story of it.

There is a great sense of rural beauty and the past in Easton but aesthetics and history were no part of my mission when I arrived at the large modern dairy unit and discovered the extent of the muddle. Two cows, for some reason best known to themselves, had decided to get into the slurry lagoon and then found themselves unable to get out of it. As you may or may not have imagined, a slurry lagoon is an agri-science euphemism for half an acre of liquid cow muck. If left to its own devices this does not smell, but disturb it and you get a very different tale altogether and its occupants had certainly

97

disturbed it. My first plan was to ask for two long poles to be procured; looking back I cannot imagine wherever I thought two such items could be found, but strangely, they materialized. The cowman and I carefully guided our charges round the edge of the lagoon towards the one place where it would be possible for them to climb out. It need hardly be said that when they arrived at this point they decided to make a further circuit. We took them round again, and again, and again. I have already admitted that those of Celtic origin are inclined to exaggerate a little but I can put my hand on my heart and say that this tale has not been ornamented. I very nearly forgot that it was Christmas, but could not help being reminded of this by the fact that we were surrounded by snow as deep, crisp and even as any Christmas carol would wish and the cold was as piercing as only the residents of East Anglia and Siberia can fully appreciate. I soon realized that I was dealing with educationally subnormal cows and that my guiding plan was going to fail. I, therefore, asked for two long ropes and again, to my surprise, these were produced. I fashioned a noose in the end of each and we attempted to lasso them. The two cows looked the nearest thing to two hippopotamuses that we should ever see in this part of Suffolk. Eyes and nostrils protruded above the surface of the slurry and, as I expertly landed the noose around the general area of a cow's head, the noose would then just lie on the surface of a liquid that was too thick to allow it to sink round the cow's neck. Still undefeated, I attempted to press the noose down with the end of the pole with which I had already armed myself but as soon as success was imminent the cow moved. We repeatedly attempted this manoeuvre and as I handled the rope and the pole the contents of the slurry lagoon gradually transferred itself to myself and I have to add to most of myself. We had been struggling with this situation for some time and had clearly failed so I considered it was time to call for a greater intellect, so summoned my partner from the bosom of his family. I was now so cold that I had passed through the pain threshold of thinking about my delicious Christmas dinner, which had almost certainly, by now, been totally demolished by my voracious family. Dick arrived with a painful show of enthusiastic advice. He decided that the answer to the whole situation lay in the procurement of a boat. I pointed out that Easton is not a seaside village, like, for example, Aldeburgh, and wondered where the hell we would find a boat in a land-locked situation such as it is. My amazement was now stretched to its utmost when the cowman said he could immediately produce one. Prior to this Christmas Day I must add that if one asked for items as commonplace as a bucket or a bar of soap, they could never be found. However, within a very short space of time a boat was indeed produced.

Dick Smith was now enjoying himself, in full command of

the rescue mission. The boat was launched with my partner as its captain and sole crew and the rest of the plan was going to be simple: he would move alongside a cow's head, place the rope over it and we would then extricate the wretched animal. The slurry was of course too liquid for anyone to walk on it but too thick for a boat to be rowed upon it. The cowman and I pushed the vessel with the aid of the long poles across the cowmuck until it reached a watery area on which it could easily float and it then drifted into the middle of this. The captain, rather surprisingly in view of the command he appeared to have of the situation when he took charge of it, had, unfortunately, no oars and we then found that our ropes were not long enough to throw to him to retrieve him.

We had been struggling for nearly three hours in the freezing cold, and inspection of the two suicidal victims showed that they were weakening and beginning to have great difficulty in keeping their noses above water. I decided that the time had come to call it a day and that the only remedy would be to shoot them in order to put them out of their misery. I set off for the hunt kennels to fetch the huntsman to perform the act of mercy, Jimmy Wickham, who I found stretched out in front of the fire and who left this particular spot with a very marked lack of enthusiasm. We soon arrived back at the disaster scene, where Dick was still marooned on the liquid sea of cow muck.

Jim's first contribution to the predicament was to express enormous hilarity at my partner's predicament. This was not appreciated by the mariner, and only a little by the rest of the party, who were too cold to appreciate anything. Jimmy's next step was to pick up a pole, tap a cow on the head with it and this, like some miracle, prompted the animal to lunge forward and walk out of the lagoon, quickly to be followed by the other. Things had now reached their lowest ebb. There was not only the freezing cold, the stinking smell and the ruined

Christmas but we now had to endure the continuous repetition of Jimmy Wickham telling us that if ever we got into any sort of muddle again, then all we had to do was send for him at an early stage and any dilemma, however difficult, would be resolved.

My own company in my car on my way home was unbearable and all the windows had to be open despite the cold. I thought I would return home to a rapturous welcome from my wife and children. My wife asked me if I realized that my lunch was totally ruined. She obviously took the view that I had been up to no good in a totally irresponsible manner on what was supposed to be a family festival and when she got near enough she insisted that I undress outside the back door before entering the family home. After a hot bath I faced an unrecognizable Christmas dinner.

A Miscellany

Cold Fair

Took place at Cold Fair Green, near Snape in December. The landlord of the Crown Inn, Westleton, used to give Westleton men hot elderberry wine and gin the night before Cold Fair.

*   *   *

Christmas Eve

To find your sweetheart to be, you put the key in the clasp of a Bible, put a garter round the Bible, rested the key on the fist, recited once a verse from the Bible relating to love and hatred

(Song of Solomon chapter 8 verses 6 and 7) then went through the alphabet and when the letter with which your future sweetheart's name began was spoken the key twisted round. Mr Brabbin did this once at a Christmas party and was 'right scared'. (J. Brabbin, fisherman).

*   *   *

Christmas

At Christmas we used to have fromenty – that's wheat boiled and eggs and sugar and spice all jumbled up together. That was at Truss Farm, Middleton (Abraham Pepper, aged 68).

Men drank fromenty at the Crown Inn, Westleton on Christmas Eve and Christmas Day up to the Great War (Joe Strowger).

· A Suffolk Christmas ·

Egg whipped up in brandy was drunk in Westleton and Middleton on Christmas morning (Abraham Pepper).

*   *   *

Letheringham

My only personal note of any worth is that my uncle (born 1904, died 1988) used to say that the high point of Christmas in my grandparents' cottage at Letheringham was when, on Boxing Night, a neighbour used to come in. They would play card games, and after some refreshment, the two men would look at each other and nod, and grandfather would fetch his screwdriver and take the stairs door off its hinges, and put it flat on the floor. Then each in turn, the two men would perform a step-dance on the wooden door, the nails from their boots striking sparks from doornails and hinges. This would have been about 1908–14, I suppose. (Gwen Dyke, 1991)

*   *   *

Before 1914 there was step-dancing in many Suffolk public houses. From Bury St Edmunds, Stowmarket and to Aldeburgh, step-dancing was a favourite pastime of the gangs of labourers. In East Suffolk, Gypsies had their own type of step-dancing. Traditional songs were sung in public houses and on festive occasions. The Ship at Blaxhall was a centre of folk music. Fiddlers and singers used to tour the villages. The Crown at Brundish, the Bell at Darsham and the Fox at Darsham had singing traditions.

*   *   *

In Suffolk the shuem'kers [shoemakers] had their own traditional holiday on the first Monday after Christmas called Shuem'kers Monday.

*   *   *

· *A Suffolk Christmas* ·

On St Thomas's Eve (20 December), in order that she might dream of the man she was to marry, a Suffolk girl had to get into bed backwards and as she did so, say:

> Good St Thomas, use me right,
> Bring to me my love this night,
> Not in gay apparel, fine array,
> But the clothes he walks in every day.

*   *   *

Aldeburgh Kitchel Cakes were triangular, spiced and currant studded. They were baked on New Year's Eve and had to be eaten before midnight or bad luck would follow.

*   *   *

Beccles Bellringers
Boxing for the chimers on the day after Christmas continued until 1899. Visitors to the tower were on one occasion invited to make contributions to the ringers by dropping money into the gotch, the large drinking vessel, that can still be seen in the ringing chamber today, and a system of forfeits for lateness or absence also supplemented the ringers' income.

*   *   *

Notice displayed one Christmas in Woodbridge store:

PLEASE ASK FOR GOODS NOT ON SALE

*   *   *

Heard in Bury St Edmunds on a Christmas Eve. First countryman to another countryman laden with shopping:-
  'Hullo, bor', You're a-doin' well. You haven't bruk yet?'
  'No, I haven't, but I'm a gettin' wholly bent.'

*   *   *

One Christmas Eve long ago Mouldy said to Chutton and Prin:

'Would yew loike ter 'arn a shillun athout a-doin' anything for't?'

'At Oi would,' replied Clutton and Prin.

'Well, dew you come along o' me,' said Mouldy and took them to the front door of the big house. Then leaving them he went round to the kitchen door and asked to see the General. He was taken to the drawing room where the General was sitting in front of a roaring fire.

'And what can I do for you?' asked the great man.

'Well, sir,' came the reply. 'Three on us ha' bin a-singin' carols outside yer front door fer the last half hour and couldn't make yer hear . . .'

'Oh dear,' said the General, putting his hand in his pocket, 'I am sorry.'

And he handed Mouldy 3s. 6d.

*   *   *

On 31 December 1900 as was their custom every Christmas time, the handbell ringers at Thornham Magna called at various houses in the village. At Thornton Hall they were invited in and given cake and beer. As they were preparing to depart their host wished all 'a very happy new century' whereupon old Fred blurted out:

'Same to you sir, and many on 'em.'

Bacon and Ham Curing

GEORGE EWART EVANS

Curing was done in a way that seems peculiar to Suffolk. The ham was first given a dry salt-bath; salt was rubbed into it and it was left in the pot, covered with salt, for seven days. At the end of this period the ham was taken out; the ham-pot was emptied of the salt and a sweet pickle was made in it. This consisted of two pounds of real black treacle; two pounds of real dark brown sugar; one quart of thick beer or stout – this, at least was Prissy Savage's formula. The beer or stout was heated and then poured over the sugar and treacle. After the ham had been thoroughly drained of the salt it would be placed in the pot and the mixture poured over it and then rubbed well into it. A big stone was then placed on top of the ham so that every part of it would be covered by the pickle. It was left in the pickle or sweet brine for about six weeks; but every day it would be turned, flesh side up one day, skin side the next. When the six weeks were up it was taken out, branded with the owners initials – a blacksmith-made iron was usually the implement – and sent off to be dried.

In the big farmhouses the hams and bacon were often dried in the huge backhouse chimney. Some distance up many of these old chimneys iron girders can still be seen running across them. From these the hams and bacon were hung. In a

farmhouse in the village of Tunstall a farmer used an eighteen or twenty stave ladder to climb up the chimney to hang his pig-meat. If one pig had been killed two hams and two chaps – the sides of the head – would be hanging from the girders drying in the wood-smoke. For only wood was burned in the backhouse fire when meat was drying.

Christmas Verses 1823

JOHN PYE and JOHN TYE

Presented to the Inhabitants of Bungay by their humble servants, the late watchmen, John Pye and John Tye.

Your pardon, Gentles, while we thus implore,
In strains and less awakening than of yore,
Those smiles we deem our best reward to catch.
And for the which we've long been on the Watch:
Well pleased, if we that recompense obtain,
Which we have ta'en so many steps to obtain,
Think of the perils in our calling past,
The chilling coldness of the midnight blast,
The beating rain, the swiftly driving snow,
The various ills that we must undergo,

· A Suffolk Christmas ·

Who roam, the glow-worms of the human race,
The living Jack-o'-Lanthorns of the place.

'Tis said by some, perchance to mock our toil,
That we are prone 'to waste the midnight oil'
And that, a task thus idle to pursue
Would be an idle waste of money too,
How hard, that we the dark designs should rue
Of those who'd fain make light of all we do,
But such the fate which oft doth merit greet,
And which now fairly drives us off our beat,
Thus it appears from this our dismal plight
That some love darkness rather than the light

Henceforth let riot and disorder reign,
With all the ills that follow in their train;
Let Toms and Jerrys unmolested brawl,
(No Charlies have they now to floor withal,)
And 'rogues and vagabonds' infest the Town,
For cheaper 'tis to save than crack a crown'.

To brighter scenes we now direct our view —
And first, fair ladies let us turn to you,
May each New Year new joys, new pleasures bring,
And life for you be one delightful spring,
No summer's sun annoy with feverish rays,
No winter chill the evening of your days.

To you kind Sirs, we next our tribute pay:
May smiles and sunshine greet you on your way,
If married, calm and peaceful be your lives;
If single, may you forthwith get you wives,

Thus, whether Male or Female, Old or Young,
Or Wed or Single, be this burden sung:
Long may you live to hear, and we to call,
A Happy Christmas and New Year to all.

Ipswich 1295

LEONARD P. THOMPSON

*For many years Leonard P. Thompson was editor of Ipswich
Blind Society's annual magazine,* Crackers. *This is an
extract from his contribution to the 1970 edition.*

The year 1295 brought to Ipswich the most colourful and exciting
Christmastide the town has probably ever known. For on 8 January
1296, Elizabeth, daughter of King Edward I, was married to the
Count of Holland in the priory church of St Peter and St Paul,
and for several days beforehand people came into the town from
miles around, to crowd the narrow streets and mingle with the
soldiers and court attendants who followed in the royal wake.

The general excitement was heightened by the influx of a
host of minstrels, dancers, fiddlers, trumpeters, citharists,
harpers, taborers, conjurors, jugglers and acrobats.

The king entered the town on the day before Christmas Eve.
Immediately his almoner distributed gifts of money to the
poor to enable them to participate in the feasting and
jollifications, and during the several days of the royal visit,
gifts were lavished on monasteries, wedding guests, and, of
course, the royal bride. Ade, the king's goldsmith, needed 'a
car with five horses' to carry coffers and panniers containing
jewels for the Lady Elizabeth from London to Ipswich.

Most of the feasting and merrymaking took place in the
'King's Hall'. The Ipswich historian, John Wodderspoon,
thought this might have been a temporary building, or

perhaps the Town House, Toll House or Meet Hall. As he said, it would of necessity have been a very large building.

The Revd C. Evelyn White, in a pamphlet on the Inns and Taverns of Ipswich, published in 1885, said it was not unlikely that the 'King's Hall' may have been the 'Sociary' which stood at the back of the Moot Hall — on the site now occupied by the Corn Exchange. He stated that this building, or one adjacent, afterwards became familiar as the King's Head from which sign King Street took its name.

We may never know whether there was any connection between the King's Hall of those Yuletide festivities in 1295 and the King's Head inn but it is certain that this was a leading Ipswich hostelry for several centuries. During the reign of King John, the inn was a halting place for the rest and refreshment of members of the Trades Guilds during their processions; and it was undoubtedly one of several Ipswich inns at which later generations of travelling entertainers amused the inhabitants.

One such showman was 'Mr Powell, the Noted Fire-Eater'. He presented his extraordinary act to an appreciative audience at the King's Head on 24 November 1750. He began by eating red-hot coals 'as naturally as bread'. For his next course he chose hot tobacco pipes — 'flaming with brimstone'. Then he took a large bunch of deal matches, lit them altogether, and held them in his mouth until the flame was extinguished. Next he drew a 'red-hot heater' from the fire, licked it, and carried it round the room between his teeth.

All this was sensational enough, but it was merely a warming up for the big moment. This is how it was described in Mr Powell's advertisement. 'He fills his mouth with red hot charcoal, and broils a slice of mutton on his tongue, and any person may blow the fire with bellows at the same time.' This was not all. Mr Powell believed in giving customers value for money. He added to his fire-eating act a 'Masquerade Dance' and — what must have been an anti-climax — 'the Diverting Humours of a Drunken Man, with Musick'.

Apt Time to Spend

THOMAS TUSSER

Many of Tusser's lines are well known but rarely credited to him.

O dirtie December,
For Christmas remember.

*　　*　　*

At Christmas play and make good cheere,
For Christmas comes but once a yeare.

*　　*　　*

At Christmas good husbands have corne on the ground,
   in barne, and in soller, woorth many a pound,
With plentie of other things, cattle and sheepe,
   all sent them (no doubt on) good houses to keepe.

At Christmas the hardnes of Winter doth rage,
   a griper of all things and specially age:
Then lightly poore people, the yoong with the old,
   be sorest oppressed with hunger and cold.

At Christmas by labour is little to get,
   that wanting, the poorest in danger are set.
What season then better, of all the whole yeere,
   thy needie poore neighbour to comfort and cheere?

Winnie's Allsorts

JOHN BURKE

John Burke was born in Sussex, brought up in Liverpool,
and spent the years of the Second World War in the UK,
France, and Belgium. After publishing and film work in
London he settled with his wife Jean in Southwold for
twenty-three years, where, he has written, 'the sun over the
rim of the world greets us before anyone else'.
He has had over a hundred books published, including
an excellent topographical one simply called Suffolk.
'Winnie's Allsorts' is based on a much-loved Southwold
character, now dead, who kept special drawers in her shop
just as in the story.

The sweetshop on the corner had been kept open every day of
the year except Christmas Day by Winnie and by her mother

before her. Sweet rationing could have made things difficult during the Second World War; but since most of the children had been evacuated to safer spots inland, demands on the Halfpenny Drawer and the Penny Drawer were less than they had been.

Those two magic drawers under the counter were an essential part of the childhood of successive generations. For a halfpenny you were allowed to choose four loose sweets from one drawer; for a penny, four rather more succulent ones from the other. And on Boxing Day each year, when the shop reopened after its brief closure, there was a free issue of 'Winnie's Allsorts' in return for a small gift from the customer: a sprig of holly or a tiny clipping from the branch of a Christmas tree . . . any little token would be accepted. It became one of the town's annual rituals: less grandiose than Santa Claus's grotto in the yard of The Schooner Hotel, but much more clearly remembered in later years by children who had grown up but never grown out of a longing for the faintly damp smell of Winnie's shop, and the alluring rattle of Winnie's Allsorts in their hiding-places. No matter how dazzling the presents on Christmas Day, there were few children who failed to dash eagerly round to the shop for their little swap the following morning.

When Winnie died, at the age of seventy-five, she left no heir or heiress. The premises were inherited by a cousin from Bury St Edmunds who did not much care for the seaside and was glad to sell off the shop for a sum which Winnie's mother and Winnie herself would have regarded as criminally extortionate. The town was becoming fashionable. The brash and the boorish were moving in to buy holiday houses, weekend houses, anything which could be tarted up and boasted about to their friends.

Simon Cheviot was twenty-eight years of age and already earning more each year on the Stock Exchange than Winnie

and her mother had made in their entire lifetimes. Within a month of buying the property he had set about converting it into a desirable coastal residence for his leisure hours. It might have been supposed that his retention of the counter and its two drawers testified to some awareness of local tradition; but in fact he thought only that it would be a nice gimmick to transform it into a breakfast bar and extend a kitchen and dining room beyond it. It made a talking point when he brought friends up from London for a weekend.

Unfortunately these friends soon found another talking point: a disagreeable one. At first they thought Simon was playing silly tricks on them and tried to laugh it off. When he claimed not to understand what they were talking about, or trying to laugh about, they grew irritated. The whole way-out thing – the noise, the scurryings, the odd little rattling sounds – became thoroughly exasperating.

'Who the hell are those kids who come through here in the mornings?'

'Kids?' Simon's bewilderment seemed genuine. 'What kids?'

Until even he became aware of it: the chattering of shrill voices, the feeling that kids were pushing past you to reach the counter. And there was a constant rattling of something inside the drawers; though when he opened them, there was only the usual array of knives and forks.

'Those brats of Simon's,' became a stock phrase among his friends – though many of them were ceasing to be friends, and found awkward excuses for not accepting further invitations.

Others, less twitchy, were glad to join him for his first Christmas at the coast. They had a happily drunken Christmas Day. But many of them were to remember Boxing Day for the worst hangover they had ever known. Excited voices buzzed in their ears. Holly scratched their wrists, and prickly pine

branches whipped their faces. There was a non-stop, enraged rattling within the kitchen drawers.

'Simon's resident poltergeists' — it started as a joke, which soon turned sour.

By midsummer a Stock Market crash had pushed Simon out of a job. He had to sell his holiday home at a considerable loss. It was bought by a Mrs Goffin who had spent her childhood in the town but left to marry in New Zealand. Now that she was back she remembered Winnie and Winnie's traditions, and planned a great Boxing Day revival. The counter was stripped of modern excrescences. Its drawers were emptied of cutlery and stocked with loose sweets. Mrs Goffin could feel the excitement throbbing in the air as the children of the past clustered around, sensing what was going to happen. Although they had all eternity to play in, they could hardly control their impatience to share their earthly memories with a new generation.

Mrs Goffin spread the word, and parents reminded their children of Winnie's Allsorts and recalled their own visits to the shop.

'Isn't it wonderful?' they enthused. 'It'll be such fun for you.'

On the morning of Boxing Day, Mrs Goffin opened the shop door and positioned herself behind the counter, occasionally opening and shutting and inspecting what had now become, through force of circumstances, the Penny Drawer and the Fivepenny Drawer. She waited. Voices whispered about her; but they were not the voices of today's children.

At last the door opened and a small boy came in, carrying the gold star from a cracker. He handed it over gravely, took his four sweets from the more expensive drawer, and turned to hurry off.

'I expect your friends will all be along soon?' said Mrs Goffin.

He paused sheepishly in the doorway. 'Well, I'm not sure.'
'Is there anything wrong?'

'Well . . . no. But . . . well, you see, there's not a lot to
bring, so they don't like to come. Most of the holly's plastic.
And the Christmas trees as well.'

'Surely not all of them. But anyway,' Mrs Goffin offered,
'tell your friends to come along just the same, and they can
have their sweets.'

'It's not just that.' He glanced at the new digital watch he
had been given for Christmas. 'There's a James Bond film on
the telly.'

He dashed away. Behind him, the children of yesterday
swirled in a disconsolate cloud around the shop, their voices
gradually fading as they accepted that it was time at last to
abandon the place which could never, ever be the same
without Winnie.

Christmas Cheer

SIR WALTER SCOTT

'Twas Christmas broached the mightiest ale;
'Twas Christmas told the merriest tale;
A Christmas gambol oft could cheer
The poor man's heart through half the year.

Snow for the Holidays

SHEILA RADLEY

Sheila Radley was born in Northamptonshire and now lives in Norfolk but her detective stories are set in Suffolk, and her likeable detective drinks beer brewed in Southwold. With her distinctive stories she now ranks among the leading present-day crime writers. This is the opening of her novel A Talent for Destruction, *first published in 1982.*

The children had never seen so much snow.

It began just in time for the start of the Christmas holidays, falling so lightly at first that it did no more than tickle their upturned faces as they ran out of school, tantalizing them with the possibility of a different world of play; snowballing in the streets, building snowmen in the gardens, toboganning in Castle Meadow, even sliding on the ice if the Mere froze over. But although the darkening sky looked full of it, and the air tasted cold and thick and still, the first fall of snow was hesitant. From the gates of the primary school, built in the expansive 1960s on the outskirts of Breckham Market, the children looked out across ploughed fields and saw with disappointment that the snow had done no more than dust the dark earth, like caster sugar sprinkled on Christmas pudding.

Fun in the snow

But that evening the wind rose, the snow beat down in a blizzard, and next morning the town – the whole of East Anglia – woke to pale empty skies and silence. Roads and paths and gardens were obliterated, houses were huddled under thick, white thatch, every telegraph and electricity line supported a narrow wall of snow. Cars that had been left outside overnight were transformed into mobile igloos. In the centre of the small town the parish church of St Botolph, standing high on the top of Market Hall, pinnacled and battlemented and soaringly Perpendicular, had been softened and rounded into lines that made it seem almost Baroque.

The children were overjoyed. They bounced outside, wellington-booted and plumped up with extra woollens and scarves, to do battle, or more peaceably to roll giant snowballs. Down by the slow black river, Castle Meadow – the site of a

120

minor twelfth-century fortification whose grassed-over ruins no archaeologist had ever found time to excavate – provided useful slopes for toboggans improvised from melamine trays and plastic fertilizer sacks. Some children hastily amended their Christmas present lists to include proper toboggans. All of them crossed their fingers in the hope that the snow would stay at least until the end of the holidays.

And the snow did stay, for weeks, bonded to the surfaces where it had fallen by exceptionally severe frosts. Ice covered the surface of the Mere to a depth of several inches, and made roads and paths hazardous. It was the hardest winter for eighteen years, a particularly difficult time for the old and infirm, for those who had to travel to work, and for farmers with livestock out in the fields.

It was a cruel winter for wild creatures, too. Emboldened by hunger, everything that flew or ran or crawled began to draw near human habitation. Mallard ducks, dispossessed from the Mere by the ice, besieged the executive houses on Mere Road. Small birds braved cats in order to snatch crumbs thrown from back doors. Backyard hens were nudged from their feeding troughs by families of rats. A fox was seen in broad daylight, scavenging round the dustbins at the back of the golf club. Only the carrion crows lived well, gorging themselves on the carcases of whatever succumbed to hunger and cold.

But for the children, the weather remained a delight. The start of the school term was an unwelcome intrusion upon their activities, because it seemed impossible that the freeze could last until the half-term holiday. Those who had managed to acquire proper toboggans felt a particular sense of frustration as they looked out of their classroom windows and saw all that snow going to waste.

Beer

GEORGE EWART EVANS

Beer was the usual drink in most households, in this parish (Blaxhall) right up to the beginning of this century (1900).

There were usually two brewings every year; one just before harvest and another in time for Christmas. Each brew took one whole day and a night. The housewife took charge; and all other jobs went by the board on this occasion as so much depended on the brew going well. The children were kept home from school to do the odd jobs about the house (at brewing time).

Journey in the Snow

ADRIAN BELL

January 1940 was a hard, cold time. In this episode from
Apple Acre, the author goes by bus from Redisham to
Beccles, a journey made longer by the detour that so many
country buses often had to make.

There is something staring, insane, about the snow. Every
man looks homeless in it. A black, lean, puppyish retriever
goes gambolling about, plunging in and out of drifts,
anybody's and everybody's dog. He follows a grey lean-nosed
woman up the road: won't be shooed away. At last, exasper-
ated, she turns and runs at him. After trudging with difficulty

so far she runs back, flapping her arms to shoo the dog. She only loses the ground she has gained. The dog thinks it a great game. She plods on again. By the time the local bus comes in sight he has grown tired of her, though, and attached himself to me. He swaggers out in front of the bus, and it pulls up with a hoot and a jerk. The driver wears a helmet like a flying man.

The bus doubles on its tracks, taking in every possible village on its way to the town. For a shilling return you see the country. You get within a mile and a half of the town – in sight of it – then round about for another four miles, coming in from another quarter.

People complain about this, but I say what's the hurry? It is a good shillingworth.

We pick up the woman who tried to chase off the dog. The door opens in a patent way. It lets in a freezing draught, so it is opened and closed every time someone gets in. 'No, not that handle: the middle one – now push.' There is a boy of about twelve in the front seat who luckily soon gets the hand of this from the driver. 'Open that door, sonny – shut the door, sonny.'

The woman with the lean Wellington nose looks out, prodding the window with it as the bus jolts, and blinking her deep-sunken eyes. What is she looking for, looking at the landscape as though it were a needle-case? Or is it just a habit?

Others get in, recognize friends, ask after each other's health, and chat. Sitting together, bouncing in unison on the same seat and chatting, with their country hats and parcelled up in their country coats. While the airman-driver charges full speed at a snowdrift in a hollow, and the bus dashes in, groans and grinds and lurches, and drags itself out on the other side like a wounded animal. The village women bounce a bit higher but do not pause in their chat.

· A Suffolk Christmas ·

*   *   *

A great red bus with steamed windows meets us – hot-looking; and we, who are only a washed-out blue, have to back. We pass a roadman, with spade shouldered, handsome – as though the crisis of the snow had knit his brow with power. The shapes of it drifted against the hedges are wild. Great sagging lips of it, a generosity of contour, a fantasy of shape, so that our gentle natured England is drowned, and the elemental forces have overwritten all, scrawled strange and foreign smiles upon the land. The skies have come down on us, and the old signs of our local life look perished and ineffectual; bits of wire-netting on stakes, fruit-trees turned to faggots – a whole fruit-farm become a few last hairs on the universal baldness.

About every mile or so some lonely figure is standing at a corner. An old man gets in with a dangerous-looking stick;

one of those old men of whom you are not sure whether they need helping or not; he looks at you as though he is looking at the distance.

'They never brought the snow-plough down my road till this morning,' he says, standing up gripping the seat in front of him. He continues to stand, as though wanting to address the whole bus. But it starts with a jolt and he is jerked into a seat.

In the snow it looks as if the old life will never resume. Does our village England sleep under that sheet – the green sward and the sleek thatch? Will the pond ruffle again and sparkle with ducks? There is something gaunt and death-like in the angular shapes of houses under the pall. A garden swing hangs stiff with its load of snow.

The snow and the war are made one now; our life is buried. And the local bus carries us through country that is no longer our country; where a roadman stands who is no longer a roadman, but carries his shovel like a weapon.

Village Poverty

GEORGE WILLIAMS FULCHER

Christmas in the 'good old days' was not so good for everyone. George Williams Fulcher (1795–1855) spent his life in Sudbury and was active in the town's politics. Village Paupers, *from which this extract is drawn, was written as a result of the Poor Law Act of 1834. The*

poem is an attack on the inhumanity and injustice of the new system and contains an angry reference to the separation of husband and wife in workhouses. The last two lines quoted refer to inmates of the workhouse which in the beginning of the poem can be identified as the one at Sudbury.

Then winter came and o'er their prospects threw
His gloomiest mantle: – pinched in food and fire,
Hope's flickering embers did at length expire,
And all the finer feelings of the Soul
Wither'd beneath their hunger's fierce countoul,
Groping 'midst refuse heaps, and things unclean,
The starving children might be daily seen,
Contending oft with loud and clam'rous cries
For rinds and parings as a costly prize,
Or roots, which from incipient decay,
The neighbouring cottagers had cast away.
Their wretched bed was all which still remained,
And for arrears of rent that was distrained,
Forth from their little cottage rudely driven,
They sought such shelter as the law had given.

Hour after hour they listless gaze, with nought
To stir the dull monotony of thought.

The Dance

MATILDA BETHAM EDWARDS

Matilda Betham Edwards (1836–1919) was a farmer's daughter. She wrote six Suffolk novels based upon personal experience. She was born and brought up on a farm at Westerfield and for a period after her father's death ran a farm near Ipswich. 'The Dance' is from A Suffolk Courtship *written in 1900.*

It begins at Christmas, the farmhouse is ready for the annual dance, the blind fiddler arrives . . .

'Ah, the fiddler's bow!'

It is difficult for modern folk to appraise that talismanic charm, the spell of the fiddle in old-world country places. Fifty years ago, music no more enlivened the farmhouse than the county jail. Pianos as yet had only found their way to mansion and rectory. A farmer's ear was attuned to rustic choruses only, to the plaintive 'come back, come back' of his guinea-fowls on the wall, to the joyous 'cluck cluck' of hens at corn-scattering, to the still more jubilant squeaking of pigs when their milk and barley-meal came in sight.

Not the bright eyes and white throats of village belles, not the punch so liberally handed round, exhilarated, nay, intoxicated so much as the sound of the fiddle. It put a convivial spirit into the dullest, emboldened the sheepish, imparted agility, if not grace, to the uncouth. No sooner had the blind fiddler fairly set things going than all present seemed to take leave of

every-day self – and every-day senses! With a jauntiness that would have made gentility blush, cavaliers now swung round their partners, lifting them off the ground, their own heels loudly beating time; alike those who knew the figures and those who did not stood up for Sir Roger de Coverley and the country dance: blunderers were noisily but good-naturedly put right, all was unsophisticated mirth and rollicking enjoyment. The bounds of propriety would of course never be over-passed under Kezia's roof. Etiquette was another matter.

Theatre Royal

Dick Whittington was the pantomime performed at the Theatre Royal, Bury St Edmunds in 1990.

The Theatre Royal was designed by William Wilkins and built in 1819. It is a rare example of a late Georgian Playhouse with fine pit, boxes and gallery.

Brandon Thomas's 'Charley's Aunt' had its first performance here with an audience of five. The farce was first produced in London at the Royalty on 21 December 1892 and ran for four years.

The Theatre Royal was used for some time as a warehouse for beer barrels, then a Restoration Trust was formed. The theatre was restored and re-decorated in the original style, predominantly in red and gold, and re-opened in the late 1960s. Since then it has gone from success to success. Its annual pantomime is always a sell-out and draws people from as far away as Ipswich, Stowmarket and Sudbury.

· *A Suffolk Christmas* ·

Dick Whittington was a Gloucestershire boy, but Suffolk has its own 'Dick Whittington' too. His name was Simon Eyre who was born at Brandon, *c.* 1395. Like Whittington, he left the country and made a fortune in London, became its Mayor and was the subject of a play performed in 1600 before Queen Elizabeth.

In 1925, the play *The Shoemaker's Holiday* was performed at the Old Vic with Edith Evans as Eyre's wife.

Dick Whittington pantomime at the Theatre Royal (*East Anglian Daily Times*)

Village Pantomime

FRANK BEARD

*Frank Beard was born at Beccles in 1911. The panto-
mime took place at Sotterley, four miles to the south of
Beccles. From a small community thirty enthusiastic people
gathered for the first rehearsal. The village schoolmistress
volunteered to produce, another woman to play the piano,
two men would be in charge of the stage carpentry, others
would paint the scenery and see to the lighting, and soon
many village women were busily making costumes . . .*

On Friday 30 January 1953 the pantomime opened for the first
of two performances, the second being at the height of the Great
Storm and North Sea surge which swept down the East Coast
with dire results. However, at eight miles from the coast, the
cast and audience were unaware of what was happening not far
away and the play went merrily on. For his part as the Court
Magician Jack had prepared an exotic-looking bowl which held,
hidden in its depths, some magnesium ribbon and a cigarette
lighter. After much patter and hocus-pocus, he plunged his
hands into the bowl, lit the ribbon, and a brilliant, smoky,
white light rose up quickly from the bowl.

An elderly lady sitting in the front 'stalls', uncomfortably close to
the stage, fell back in alarm. Her chair went back too far and she
landed in the lap of the man behind. When the unsympathetic
laughter at the lady's discomfiture had died down, the Court
Magician recovered his composure and the play went on.

Many villages round about vied with each other in offering facilities to receive the pantomime after its fame had spread far and wide. However, the lot fell upon Ilketsall St Andrews and *The Sleeping Beauty* duly arrived with all its paraphernalia, including some more magnesium ribbon. The men's dressing room in the garden at the back of the hall, consisted of four posts with a covering of tarpaulin resting somewhat crazily across the tops. All went well until nearly the end of the first act. The Court Magician accompanied by the hefty Court Jester and the still heftier Court Cook were doing their dance number when the stage could bear it no longer. The 'dancers' floundered into a confused heap and the audience roared their approval of this unrehearsed 'spot' in the pantomime. The act was declared ended. Men in the audience hurried out to fetch barrels from the pub next door and make a hasty repair, resting the staging on the barrels. There was no more dancing but the show went on to a joyous conclusion.

Sweet Suffolk Owl

ANON

Sweet Suffolk Owl, so trimly dight
With feathers, like a lady bright,
Thou sing'st alone, sitting at night
    Te Whit! Te Whoo!   Te Whit! Te Whit!

Thy note that forth so freely rolls
  with shrill commands the mouse controls,
And sings a dirge for dying souls
      Te Whit! Te Whoo!   Te Whit! Te Whit!

Christmas Soliloquy

LEONARD P. THOMPSON

In this nostalgic piece (from Crackers, *1972) the author recalls his childhood Christmases in Ipswich. The years pass, but here Mr Thompson shows that Christmas lasts for ever, or, to quote Charles Dickens, 'Happy, happy Christmas, that can win us back to the delusions of our childhood days'.*

This Christmastide of 1971 began for me at 3 o'clock this afternoon, when the radio broadcast of *A Festival of Nine Lessons and Carols from King's College Chapel, Cambridge*, opened with that marvellous singing of 'Once in Royal David's City'. Now, as I look across the quiet fields, a patch of light pinpoints a distant cottage. In the village, which I cannot see, other lights will now be shining through the gathering December dusk.

For the village shops the day is drawing to a close, but it has by no means ended for the village inn where tonight, as on the nights of many other Christmas Eves, there will be a warmth and cheerfulness such as will be found in similar establishments throughout the land. And at the end of this day the lights will go up in the village church, and people will make their way towards it, to remember with gladness that other inn in the stable of which the Christmas Story began so long ago at Bethlehem.

Although I live in the country now, and my ancestors for many generations lived by farming, I am no countryman. This

afternoon, as the Christmas peace settles over the countryside, my thoughts are among the bright shops and well-lit pavements of Ipswich, where I was born and where I spent a happy childhood. And gradually, as darkness enfolds the country scene that is framed by my study window, the curtains of memory part, and all that belongs to the late afternoon of this Christmas Eve of 1971 dissolves into the sights, sounds and smells of another Christmas Eve of long ago.

The family home is filled with all the warmth, brightness and rich promise of Yuletide festivity. A decorated Christmas Tree stands in the square hall. Pictures have been crowned with sprigs of holly, and mistletoe hangs over doors. Coloured paper garlands festoon the walls and ceilings of dining- and drawing-rooms. Christmas cards stand on mantelpieces and the piano, around which we shall sing the old beloved carols. Tomorrow there may be more cards and perhaps a parcel or two, for there will be two postal deliveries on Christmas Day.

It was the postman who, four or five weeks ago, brought us

The Southwold Railway

the always eagerly awaited foretastes of this wonderful season of goodwill and gifts. They were the marvellous Christmas catalogues issued by W.S. Cowell Limited of Ipswich, and A.W. Gamage Limited of Holborn. Each having many illustrations and several exciting pages devoted to toys. And of course there have also been the waits and carol singers reminding us, on several evenings during the past fortnight that Christmas was drawing near.

The day has been one of exciting preparations. The turkey has been plucked, and this morning I performed my usual task of wrenching brussels sprouts from their stalks: it is a job I do not like on cold days, but in helping my mother I have to take the rough with the smooth, and earn my pocket money. I found pleasure in polishing the brass fire irons and fenders with Brasso, and satisfaction in burnishing table knives with bath-brick on the knife board. I did not mind going on an errand to the drapery establishment of Messrs. Bell and Barr, where I accepted a packet of pins in lieu of a farthing change. I galloped most of the way there and back, for I went on my imaginary horse.

Rich odours fill the house. Father has been given a prime Suffolk ham, and it is boiling in the large, oval, iron vessel in which, a week or so ago, the Christmas puddings were boiled. Within a few minutes mince pies and sausage rolls will be taken from the oven. I shall be allowed to sample one of each, piping hot. Mother has also made some rich shortbread and round, flat biscuits which she decorates with glace cherries and slivers of angelica, and calls 'Shrewsburys'.

Father has come home, and I help him to re-arrange furniture in readiness for the large family party which will assemble tomorrow. A little before seven o'clock Aunt Sue arrives. She is always full of fun, and my little sister and I greet her excitedly. We regard her as having made a tremendously adventurous journey, for she has come by train all the way from Colchester.

· *A Suffolk Christmas* ·

Now it is time for bed. As is customary on Christmas Eve in our home, fires are blazing in the bedrooms. I am too excited to sleep, indeed I am resolved to stay awake. Father Christmas, in whom I firmly believe, is due to visit our house some time during the night and I am determined to see him. Snug in my bed, I lie watching the rosy flicker of firelight on walls and ceiling, as I await the bearer of presents. Sleep overtakes me, and when I awake, the fire is out and the room is filled with pale cold moonlight.

Gently, I move my feet, and there is the soft rustle of paper. He has been! And I did not see him! I get out of bed, and look through a window. Moonlight is shining through bare trees, and on the frosted roofs of houses on the other side of the road. I listen for the sound of sleigh bells, but the night is still. I climb back into bed and with my fingers I tentatively explore the shapes of two or three parcels, and the outline of the bulging stocking which lies across the foot of the bed. My mother's voice comes from the next room. 'Go to sleep. It's only half-past four.'

I close my eyes and count up to one hundred. I open them, and it is still moonlight. I repeat this exercise, again, and again. I awake. It is daylight! Where shall I start? On a parcel? Or that long, black present-crammed stocking? Experience tells me that the heel will probably be stuffed with an orange. I feel; it is. I also expect that half-way down the leg there will be a box of Tunis dates to which I am partial. Again I feel; yes, there is. I take a paper bag from the top, and find that it contains two sugar mice, one pink, one white, they have tails of string.

Next there is a small, shining, white tin motor car, a splendid toy which has been made in Germany and bought for a few pennies. Another toy is an acrobat on a bar fixed between two strips of wood, which, when pressed together, set the performer in motion. I turn to the parcels. I unwrap a book,

137

· A Suffolk Christmas ·

The Swiss Family Robinson; it has a stiff cover and its many beautiful illustrations include four full-paged colour plates. Then I select a red, oblong box; I lift the lid to reveal eight shining Guardsmen, resplendent in scarlet tunics and black bearskins, and in the centre is their officer, mounted on a white horse.

After unwrapping a slate, a game of Ludo, and a Jack-in-the-box, I return to the stocking. I find slate pencils, crayons, a pencil box, chocolate cigarettes and nuts. I have left the largest parcel until last. It is a young postman's outfit, and it includes a hat with peaks at front and back (a Shako) which I proudly think is rather like the one my Uncle Harry wears.

I wear my postman's shako as I tuck into my breakfast ham, keeping an eye on the window for the coming of the real postman, until, at last, there he is, Uncle Harry himself, delivering letters at a house across the road. Then he comes to us, and we all go to the door to wish him a happy Christmas. My plea to be allowed to go with him on his round is rejected, so I stay at home, still wearing my shako, and pass the morning parading my soldiers, manipulating my acrobat, 'smoking' one or two of my chocolate cigarettes, eating a few dates, and in no way impairing my appetite for the feast ahead.

Towards one o'clock the family party assembles. Another aunt, two uncles, two cousins, and my paternal grandmother, who will spend much of the day in an armchair by the fire, smiling contentedly on all that is happening around her, and thinking, perhaps, of the Christmases of the childhood years she passed in an Essex inn in the middle years of the nineteenth century.

I begin my Christmas dinner with a golden island of batter pudding in a brown sea of rich gravy, and in due course I partake of Christmas pudding. I do not really want it but there is the possibility that I will find a silver threepenny piece – perhaps even a silver sixpence. The dining-room windows are

clouded by steam, veiling a world in which a great many other children have no Christmas dinner. I give a passing thought to that 'poor little boy in the street' to whom my mother has sometimes threatened to give my dinner on days when I have been reluctant to eat it. This is an age in which some people believe that a child must be persuaded to eat as much as possible to make it grow big and strong, but when too many have so little opportunity for so doing.

The day wears on, and seems to be devoted largely to feasting. Oranges, apples, nuts, dates, figs, crystalized fruits, chocolates – dishes and boxes are passed round and round. Then a massive tea. No one appears to be in imminent danger of fainting from hunger, but tradition has to be observed. The table is loaded with bread and butter, mince pies, sausage rolls, jelly, blancmange, a chocolate log which is very rich and has been obtained – as always – from Mr William Thompson's confectionery establishment in Tavern Street. I think it would be nice to have him for a relation, which he is not. There is also my mother's Christmas cake and the inevitable tall glass jars of crisp celery. It is fortunate that there has been frost, otherwise it would not be considered 'nutty'. And of course there are crackers, each contains a coloured paper hat, a trinket or a small puzzle, and a 'motto'.

We withdraw to the other room whilst the table is being relaid for supper which will include a splendid Melton Mowbray pork pie which a friend of my father's sends him every year from Leicester, and we play games. Consequences, How, When and Where, Twilight, Blind Man's Buff, and Charades. Then there is the tail-less donkey, his picture is pinned to a board, and blind-folded we take turns to pin a tail on him, with some very comical results. We sing carols.

The entire programme – Christmas dinner, tea, supper, games and all, will be repeated tomorrow when we visit the household of those who have visited us today.

Harry Becker (1865–1928) vividly recorded scenes of rural
Suffolk in a variety of mediums during his life in East
Bergholt, Wenhaston and finally Hinton

To Suffolk

CECIL LAY

Cecil Lay (1885–1956) was the son of the village schoolmaster at Aldringham. An architect by profession, he lived nearly all his life in Aldringham, the last part of his poem 'To Suffolk' which is quoted here states that Suffolk knew the reason.

When pool and stream were frozen hard,
And cattle stayed within the yard;
When elms were red, and ash-trees black,
And sparrows robbed the farmer's stack;
When tilth and fallow changed to stone,
And hoodies fought around a bone;
When hands were numb and minds depressed,
When snow the naked trees had dressed,
   Said I, I will away from here
   In this hard season of the year

   Yet here I stay and years go by
   And Suffolk knows the reason why.

Acknowledgements

Christmas 1863 by Clifford Morsley, first published in *East Anglian Magazine*, quoted by permission of the author. Christmas Market, extract from *Corduroy* by Adrian Bell, first published by Cobden Sanderson, 1930, and permission granted by the late Mrs Marjorie Bell. Seasonal Fare and Handbells, quoted from *Spoken History* by George Ewart Evans, published by Faber & Faber 1987, by permission of the publishers. Ploughing, extract from *Farm Down The Lane* by B.A. Steward, published by Claude Morris 1946, quoted by permission of the author. Christmas is Seldom White, *East Anglian Daily Times*, 1962, by permission of the Editor. Tragedy at Sea, extract from *Sophia's Son* by Dorothy Thompson, published by Terence Dalton Ltd, 1975, by permission of the publishers. *A Southwold Christmas* by Lyn Knights, 1991, by permission of the author. Ghost in the Garden, from *East Anglian Tales*, by H. Mills West, published by Countryside Books, 1990, and used by permission of the publisher. Seasonal Customs by Clifford Morsley, first published by *Eastern Daily Press*, used by permission of the author. Coaching Days, extract from *Suffolk Coaching Days* by Leonard P. Thompson, published by Peake Publications, 1966, and quoted by permission of Mrs E.O. Thompson. Green Lane Farm in the 1940s, extract from *Green Lane Farm* by B.A. Steward, published by Farming Press 1982, and used by permission of the author and publisher. A Lowestoft Christmas, by permission of the *Lowestoft Journal*. Nativity Play at Hollesley Colony, extract from *Borstal Boy* by Brendan Behan, published by Hutchinson 1958, and used by permission of the publisher. *Christmas Chaos* by John Waller, MS 1991, quoted by permission of the author. Carol Singers, extract from *A Street in Suffolk*, by Adrian Bell, published by Faber & Faber 1964, and used by permission of the late Mrs Marjorie Bell. *Carolling with Benjamin Britten and Peter Pears*, by Barbara Brook, MS 1991, by permission of the author. The Garden, extract from *In a Green Shade*, by Doreen Wallace, published by Lutterworth Press 1950, and quoted by permission of David Higham Associates. Christmas Eve 1938, extract from *Green Grow the Rushes* by Peter Gerrell, published by Tyndale & Panda Publishing 1987, and quoted by permission of the publisher. Party Bells, extract from *A Peacock on the Lawn* by Anna Hadfield, published by Hutchinson 1965, and quoted by permission of John Hadfield. Yuletide at Debenham, extract from *Reminiscences of Country Life* by James Cornish, first published by *Country Life* 1939. A Woman's Point of View, *East Anglian Daily Times*, by permission of the Editor. Christmas Candles 1939, extract from *Apple Acre* by Adrian Bell, first published by The Bodley Head 1942, by permission of the late Mrs Marjorie Bell. An American's Wartime Christmas, extract from *Here We Are Together* by Robert Arbib, published by Longmans 1946, quoted by permission of the publisher. Entertaining POWs, extract from *Peter Howard, Life and Letters* by Anne Wolridge Gordon, published by Hodder & Stoughton 1969, quoted by permission of the publisher. *A Vet's Christmas Day*, by Philip Ryder-Davies, MS 1991, by permission of the author. Bacon and Ham Curing, extract from *Ask the Fellows who cut the Hay* by George Ewart Evans, published by Faber, quoted by permission of the late Mrs Marjorie Bell. Ipswich 1295, extract from article by Leonard P. Thompson, first published in *Crackers* 1970, used by permission of Mrs E.O. Thompson. *Winnie's Allsorts* by John Burke, MS 1991, by permission of the author. Snow for the

Holidays, extract from *A Talent for Destruction* by Sheila Radley, published by Constable 1982, used by permission of the author and publisher. Beer, extract from *Ask the Fellows who cut the Hay* by George Ewart Evans, published by Faber, quoted by permission of the publisher. Journey in the snow, extract from *Apple Acre* by Adrian Bell, first published by The Bodley Head 1942, by permission of the late Mrs Marjorie Bell. Village Pantomime, extract from *My Childhood in Suffolk* by Frank Beard, published by the author and used by his permission. Christmas Soliloquy by Leonard P. Thompson, published in *Crackers* 1972, permission by Mrs E.O. Thompson.

If, inadvertently, copyright material has been included for which I have failed to obtain permissions, or I have failed to give thanks where they are due, I tender my sincere apologies which I hope will be accepted.

Some friends have written pieces especially for this anthology; Mrs Barbara Brook, Mr John Burke, Mrs Lyn Knights, Mr Philip Ryder-Davies and the Revd John Waller. For their generosity I am deeply grateful, as I am to all who have assisted in so many other ways.

Picture Credits

R. Wright, pp. x, 70; original illustration by Doreen Wallace, H. Phelps, p. 2; H. Phelps, pp. 7, 10; D. Oliver, p. 12; Dunwich Museum, p. 14; *East Anglian Daily Times*, pp. 16, 65, 130; Middleton Community Council, pp. 21, 76; J. Smith, pp. 23, 27; J. Tooke, pp. 25, 31, 42, 55, 56, 135; A.J. Errington, p. 37; original illustration by Brian Walker, Brian Walker, p. 46; D. Kindred, p. 53; Mrs Platt, p. 60; N. Walker, p. 78; Adnams Brewery, pp. 82, 109; Mrs Gissing, p. 120; original illustration by Harry Becker, P. Loftus, p. 140.